"If there were a literary avant-garde that were relevant now, it would be what the queers and their allies are doing, at the intersections, across disciplines. This avant-garde would be inclusive, racially and culturally diverse, migrants galore, predominately but not exclusively working-class, transdisciplinary, (gender)queer and politically clued up (left)." Isabel Waidner

*Liberating the Canon* is an anthology capturing the contemporary emergence of radically innovative and nonconforming literatures in the UK and beyond. Historically, sociopolitical marginalisation and avant-garde aesthetics have not come together in UK literature, counterintuitively divorcing outsider experience and formal innovation. Bringing together intersectional identity and literary innovation, *LTC* is designed as an intervention against the normativity of literary publishing contexts and the institution 'Innovative Literature' as such. More widely, if literature, any literature, can act as a mode of cultural resistance and help imagine a more progressive politics in Tory Britain and beyond, it is this.

Contributors work at the intersections of prose, poetry, art, performance, indie publishing and various subcultural contexts: Mojisola Adebayo, Jess Arndt (US), Jay Bernard, Richard Brammer, Victoria Brown, Steven J. Fowler, Juliet Jacques, Sara Jaffe (US), Roz Kaveney, R. Zamora Linmark (US), Mira Mattar, Seabright D. Mortimer, Nat Raha, Nisha Ramayya, Rosie Šnajdr, Timothy Thornton, Isabel Waidner, Joanna Walsh and Eley Williams.

# Liberating The Canon:

## An Anthology of Innovative Literature

### Edited by Isabel Waidner

**Dostoyevsky Wannabe Experimental**
*An Imprint of Dostoyevsky Wannabe*

First Published in 2018
by Dostoyevsky Wannabe Experimental
All rights reserved
All copyright reverts to the individual authors

Dostoyevsky Wannabe Experimental is an imprint of Dostoyevsky
Wannabe publishing.

Cover design by Victoria Brown
dostoyevskywannabe.com

ISBN-13:978-1999924508
ISBN-10:1999924509

# CONTENTS

INTRODUCTION                 7
JULIET JACQUES              21
ELEY WILLIAMS               33
MOJISOLA ADEBAYO            41
ISABEL WAIDNER              61
ROSIE ŠNAJDR               73
STEVEN J. FOWLER           79
JOANNA WALSH               91
JAY BERNARD               105
TIMOTHY THORNTON          111
JESS ARNDT                121
MIRA MATTAR               143
VICTORIA BROWN            157
NISHA RAMAYYA             165
SEABRIGHT D. MORTIMER     173
RICHARD BRAMMER           179
NAT RAHA                  193
SARA JAFFE                205
ROZ KAVENEY               215
R. ZAMORA LINMARK         233

CONTRIBUTORS              265

## LIBERATING THE CANON: INTERSECTIONALITY AND INNOVATION IN LITERATURE

i.

*Liberating the Canon* (Dostoyevsky Wannabe, 2018) is an edited anthology capturing the contemporary emergence of nonconforming and radically innovative literatures in the UK and beyond. Historically, sociopolitical marginalisation and avant-garde aesthetics have not come together in UK literature, counterintuitively divorcing outsider experience and formal innovation. Bringing together intersectionality[1] and literary innovation, *Liberating the Canon* (*LTC*) is designed as an intervention against the normativity of literary publishing contexts and the institution 'Innovative Literature' as such. This is *how* we redo canonical: We don't just work across the identity categories (BAME, LGBTQI, woman, working-class) and their various intersections. (We don't just put our difference to work.) We also work across formal distinction (prose and poetry, and various genre distinctions) and across disciplines (literature, art, performance, critical theory and various subcultural contexts), unrepressing what the cultural theorist Raymond Williams termed the "multiplicity of writing".[2] What does that mean and why does it matter, I'll get back to it.

When I started editing the anthology in Autumn '17, I did not expect the level of support the project would be met with. All but one of the writers I invited agreed to contribute original and previously unpublished work (in print), foregoing

1 Intersectionality is the theory that various systems of oppression intersect to create social identities that are different from the component identities. The term was coined by Kimberlé Bradshaw in 1989.

2 Williams, Raymond (1977) *Marxism and Literature*. Oxford: Oxford University Press p.146. Williams wrote that formal and disciplinary limitations suppressed the multiplicity of writing at the still active and shaping stage.

any commissioning fee or payment.[3] Joanna Walsh (me, emailing). I'm editing an anthology of innovative literature for Dostoyevsky Wannabe, the Manchester-based independent press. The idea is to capture the ongoing emergence of innovative and nonconforming forms of writing in the UK, and to make connections to likeminded US literatures. I'm hardly in the position to ask you contribute. There is no budget. Dostoyevsky Wannabe work with a nonprofit publishing ethos, that is, they sell their books via Amazon at cost price in order to make them affordable to as broad a readership as possible. Publishers, designer, editor and authors are working for free, and mostly without institutional support. The aim is to produce books that challenge literary conventions, and to precipitate the ongoing disruption of the British publishing establishment. Anyway, I'm writing an intro about the relationship between marginalised identity (BAME, LGBTQI, women, working-class, at the intersections) and formal innovation in literature. The way they have not gone together in UK literature until now. You wouldn't consider endorsing the book? Naw (Walsh, replying). I'd love to contribute! I'm occasionally writing stories toward a collection that might be ready in a year or two, so this gives me the impetus to finish one of them (end, Walsh). South London playwright, director and performer Mojisola Adebayo agreed to contribute the first part of her forthcoming play, titled *Stars*. According to Adebayo, "*Stars* is a play with animation and music that tells the story of an old lady who travels into outer space... in search of her own orgasm. The play poetically explores the power and politics of pleasure for women, girls and intersex people. It questions why millions of people are prevented from being able to reach the heights of sexual pleasure as a result of sexual trauma and genital mutilation practices, traditions and surgical interventions that continue to this day on every continent, and connects all these themes with space travel." Combining a

3 Many writers and publishers committed to challenging literary conventions and the exclusiveness of the publishing establishment have been prepared to work outside of the paying economy in order to effect change. This, too, needs to change (free labour).

situated politics (based on personal and professional experience, and research), and genre-crossing, culturally hybrid, formally innovative writing, Adebayo's *Stars* is doing exactly the kind of literary work that needs doing now. Steven J. Fowler (me again). I'm editing an anthology. Would you like to contribute a piece of writing like *MueuM*, the fiction that was short-listed for The White Review Short Story Prize in 2014? I <3 *MueuM*. Have this unpublished prose piece, titled *The Bassment Gallery* (Fowler, on email). It's a bit brutal (end, Fowler). *The Bassment Gallery* quotes bisexual Polish absurdist Witold Gombrowicz (1904-1969), is littered with 'spelling mistakes', and is doing exactly the kind of literary work that needs doing now. Or, Roz Kaveney (hi). You wouldn't want to contribute something like *Tiny Pieces of Skull*, your pioneering novel depicting the transgender experience in London and Chicago in the early '80s. Long shot, I know. I want to situate the writers of now as part of a longer genealogy of outsider writing (end, my email). Written in 1988, Kaveney's *Tiny Pieces of Skull* was admired by contemporaries including Kathy Acker in manuscript. It received the attention of two publishers at the time, who ended up passing it on as too risqué. It did not find a publisher until London-based Team Angelica put it out in 2015. *Tiny Pieces of Skull* went on to win a Lambda Literary Award for best trans fiction in the same year. Do you want the abortive sequel to *Tiny Pieces*? It's never been published (Kaveney, replying). Some of it may be a bit TMI [too much information] (end, Kaveney). She sent me *Cream Whip*, a fictional or autobiographical account of the rarely written about practicalities of dilation (the use of a dilator to prevent a new vagina from closing after gender reassignment surgery). Finally, Nat Raha (me, emailing). Thanks for the invitation (Raha, responding)! The project sounds great and very much aligned to the kind of editorial work that I feel most strongly about right now (end, Raha). I could go on. Project *Liberating the Canon*, as it was not then called, touched a nerve. It is a project shared by many.

*LTC* is not just an intervention against the normativity of innovative publishing contexts in the UK. If literature, any literature, should be relevant now, it must have the potential to help counteract the rise of conservativism, nationalism and similarly divisive ideologies and policy-making. In a 'post-truth' sociopolitical context where powerful narratives and metaphors shape public opinion and influence electoral results, fictions and literary imaginaries must aim to advance a more progressive politics within marginalised communities and beyond, and to act as a mode of cultural resistance. In order to ensure that this kind of work can be written and published, what counts as literary innovation has got to change.

ii.

Asked about the lack of diversity in the publishing industry in 2015, Black British publishing pioneer and diversity campaigner Margaret Busby spoke of the bore of having to address the same topic for 30 years.[4] Despite good intentions and ongoing initiatives to diversify (such as Penguin's WriteNow, a mentoring programme for new writers from underrepresented communities), literary publishing (and literature itself) in the UK remain bastions of class and exclusiveness in 2018. But if literary publishing is bad, innovative (or experimental, or avant-garde) publishing is worse.[5] Literary innovation has been the prerogative of the white middle-class patriarchy (to call a spade a spade), whereas the rest of us have been writing, what, memoir or romcom. Genre fiction. As if by coincidence, commercial

4    https://www.theguardian.com/books/2015/dec/11/how-do-we-stop-uk-publishing-being-so-posh-white-male. For a recent take, see Arifa Akbar, "Diversity in publishing - still hideously middle-class and white?" in *The Guardian*, 9 December 2017, https://www.theguardian.com/books/2017/dec/09/diversity-publishing-new-faces?

5 For example, Cathy Park Hong, "Delusions of Whiteness in the Avant-Garde," in *Lana Turner Journal of Poetry*, Issue 7, 3 November 2013, http://www.lanaturnerjournal.com/7/delusions-of-whiteness-in-the-avant-garde. Or Juliana Spahr and Stephanie Young, *foulipo*, talk for CalArts Noulipo conference, 28–29 October 2005, http://www.drunkenboat.com/db8/oulipo/feature-oulipo/essays/spahr-young/foulipo.html.    Or Lauren Elkin (2013) 'Oulipo Lite', in *The End of Oulipo? An Attempt to Exhaust a Movement*. London: Zero Books, pp.66-99.

publishing categories map exactly onto historical high and low culture distinctions. Literature, by definition, is high culture. The rest is chick lit, sci-fi, speculative fiction, you name it. The ways in which distinctions between high and low culture have operated to marginalise BAME, LGBTQI, working-class and women writers have been theorised in the field of British cultural studies since its inception in the 1950s. Accordingly, genre distinctions, in particular the distinction between literary fiction (high culture) and genre fiction (low culture), are structures that actively but implicitly reproduce the literary canon in its exclusiveness and normativity.

Most of the texts included in *LTC* are displacing genre categories. They work across (classist) high and low culture distinctions. Juliet Jacques's acclaimed *Trans: A Memoir* (Verso's title) combines trans history, queer theory and autobiography to produce a quite different kind of memoir, not unlike US writer Maggie Nelson's *The Argonauts* (2015) combines gender theory with personal accounts of queer pregnancy and filmmaker Harry Dodge's (Nelson's partner) top surgery. *The Holiday Camp* (Jacques, this volume) is a short fiction about teenager Sam's first experiments with drag in the context of the titular British holiday camp. Against a backdrop of provincial transphobic and homophobic bullying (gaylord, bender, and my personal favourite "*Are you a girl or a boy?*"), Sam (in drag) takes herself to the ball (so to speak), even if the ball is in Reigate, Surrey. Jacques may or may not have enrolled autobiographical elements (she didn't say). But I'd be surprised if anyone wrote homophobia and closeted longing as well this if they hadn't experienced it. In *Never the Blade* (this volume), Mira Mattar splices a history of the pink plastic flamingo (from the working class lawns of the 1950s, via John Waters, to Primark and Prada), and a reflection on unbelonging, weddedness, unweddedness, hen parties, love and the unruliness of the body. While Jess Arndt's *Serape* (in *LTC*) is a straight (not) fiction set during the Gold Rush time period in San Francisco, *Deep Desert* (also in LTC) is an autofiction or interior travelogue written during their time living in the Mojave Desert. And *Fantômas Takes Sutton* (Waidner, *LTC*) refracts my real-life sojourn in suburban Sutton through a pro-active reading of

Julio Cortázar's 1975 pamphlet *Fantômas Versus the Multinational Vampires* (reissued by Semiotext(e) in 2014). Cortázar wrote his *Fantômas* in response to having attended the Second Russell Tribunal in '73, an international committee investigating human-rights abuses in Latin America. At the time I was writing the first draft of my *Fantômas*, the Conservative Party under David Cameron had just been elected for a second term, paving the way for the consequential EU referendum in 2016. I did not know then the result of the Brexit vote, but I did know that the dismantling of social security and disability rights under the Tory leadership had been termed a humanitarian catastrophe by the UN. In this context, *Fantômas Takes Sutton* imagines myself and a non-closeted, gender nonconforming version of Julio Cortázar spearheading a suburban counter-austerity avant-garde.

The extent to which British innovative literature intersects with international genealogies is a question worth raising. For example, New Narrative is a movement and theory of queer and working-class avant-garde writing which emerged in the US and Canada from the 1970s onwards and which is currently experiencing a resurgence in the US and also the UK.[6] Not only did New Narrative converge high culture (literary experimentalism) and low culture (pop and subcultural references, sex and gossip). Like other US and Canadian literatures, New Narrative also made headway towards displacing distinctions between prose and poetry, critical and creative writing, and the short story and novel forms. Why were these distinctions preserved in the UK for so long, and to what effects? Jay Bernard, Steven J. Fowler, Mira Mattar, Timothy Thornton and Eley Williams write both, prose and poetry. Arguably, everything they write is somewhere in between. Joanna Walsh's *I Wish Someone Loved Me That Isn't Capitalism* (in *LTC*) is an exposition on sex and class, in short

6 Dodie Bellamy & Kevin Killian (eds.) (2017) *Writers Who Love Too Much: New Narrative Writing 1977-1997*. New York: Nightboat Books. Gail Scott, Robert Glück, Camille Roy and Mary Burger, (eds.) (2004) *Biting the Error: Writers Explore Narrative*. Toronto: Coach House Books. See also Eileen Myles & Liz Kotz (eds.) (1999) *The New Fuck You: Adventures in Lesbian Reading*. Los Angeles: Semiotext(e)/MIT Press.

lines. Although New Narrative texts were circulating on the LGBTQI London art scene since the mid '90s at least, they did not shape the wider literary landscape in Britain until fairly recently. At present, British publishers are (re)issueing form and genre-defying work from the US (Eileen Myles's *Chelsea Girls* (Serpent's Tail, 1994/2016), Maggie Nelson's *The Argonauts* (Melville House, 2016), Chris Kraus's *I Love Dick* (Serpent's Tail, 1997/2015), or Michelle Tea's *Black Wave* (And Other Stories, 2017)), but their output of British fictions remains comparably normative and often mainstream.

*LTC* aims to fortify connections between contemporary innovative literatures in the UK and likeminded US literatures. We might be an island but influence travels. (Influence *should* travel.) One of the contributors to this volume is Filipino-American New Narrative writer R. Zamora Linmark. *Rolling the R's* (Linmark, 1997) has justifiably acquired the status of a cult novel. It features a Farah Fawcett Fan Club and examines gayness and the South East Asian diasporic experience in 1970s Honolulu, Hawaii. Also tackling LGBTQI politics at the intersections, Linmark's contribution to *LTC*, *Dear Jesus*, is a series of letters (prayers) responding to the legalisation of gay marriage in Hawaii in 2013. But beyond intersecting UK/US avant-garde genealogies and transatlantic exchange, the version of Britishness staged in *LTC* is already culturally hybrid. Mojsola Adebayo uses West-African story telling techniques (grioting) to problematise closeted lesbianism on a South London council estate. Steven J. Fowler's work draws on the East European avant-gardes (his experimental play *Mayakovsky* (2017) explored the life and death of the Russian poet, for example). Nisha Ramayya's contribution, *Fainting Away*, is part of *States of the Body Produced by Love* (forthcoming), a series of responses to states of being British-Indian, in relation to the colonial and postcolonial states of Britain and India. And I am a working-class LGBTQI European migrant and non-native English writer. This is the kind of Britain we are (this is 2018).

iii.

As well as formal distinctions, Raymond Williams wrote that disciplinary limitations suppressed the multiplicity of writing. As a matter of fact, most contemporary authors writing literatures which combine marginalised identity and formal innovation have come through disciplines other than literature, and/or they are working with a transdisciplinary orientation. Mojisola Adebayo's plays fuse history, politics, drama, poetry, autobiography, fact and fiction, much like New Narrative writing by Dodie Bellamy, Kevin Killian, Robert Glück or Renee Gladman has done in a US literature context. Jay Bernard is a writer and poet, but also a programmer for BFI FLARE (the London LGBTQI film festival) and an interdisciplinary artist. Joanna Walsh is a writer and illustrator (she drew the cover art for Jacques' *Trans: A Memoir*, for example). Richard Brammer is a writer, publisher and co-founder of Dostoyevsky Wannabe (with Victoria Brown), self-taught computer coder and ex-NHS-laboratory worker (an experience fictionalised in his 2017 chapbook *The End of History*). Victoria Brown is a working-class poet, world-class designer and co-founder of Dostoyevsky Wannabe. She is also full-time in data administration for the Probation Service. Juliet Jacques has a background in criticism (she wrote a book about the novelist Rayner Heppenstall) and journalism (her memoir started out as a Guardian blog). She is currently making a name for herself as an experimental filmmaker. I came to literature via music. Lastly with the indie band Klang, I released records on UK labels Rough Trade (2003) and Blast First (2002). *LTC* contributor Sara Jaffe's band, San Francisco-based Erase Errata, and Klang toured together in '03. Jaffe was writing a tour diary at the time. In 2016, she released her debut novel *Dryland* (Tin House) to critical acclaim. Her contribution to this volume, the short narrative *Baby in a Bar*, deals with the subtle awkwardness of transitioning into queer parenting. It is through Jaffe that I heard of Jess Arndt, co-founder (with Jaffe) of US indie New Herring Press and third and final US contributor to *LTC*. "Wildly original" (to quote from Maggie Nelson's blurb), Arndt's collection *Large Animals* (Catapult, 2017) problematises transdisciplinary subjects including the simultaneous openness and containment of (queer) bodies, human animal relationality and the pain of the editing process.

Why, then, are most contemporary, politically acute avant-garde writers coming through poetry, performance, art, film, you name it, and not prose literature? Let's take as an example just *one* of the many exclusions where identity and innovation failed to coalesce in UK literature: queer avant-garde fiction. Queer and trans avant-garde performance (Travis Alabanza, David Hoyle, Le Gateau Chocolat, Scottee, Victoria Sin), film (John Akomfrah, Campbell X), art (Richard Dodwell, Evan Ifekoya, Charlotte Prodger), photography (Christa Holka, Jacob Love, Holly Revell), and more recently poetry (Jay Bernard, Steven J. Fowler, Nat Raha, Sophie Robinson, Timothy Thornton) are positively THRIVING in contemporary Britain. In contrast, there is hardly any queer avant-garde fiction. Neither has there been a significant tradition: historically, British queer experimental novels are scarce (Brigid Brophy's *In Transit* (1969) and Maureen Duffy's *The Microcosm* (1966) are exceptions). And despite their popularity, Ali Smith's subtly experimental novels have yet to pave the way for more radically queer (or BAME, or working-class) literary experimentation. So why are queerness and experimentation thriving in British poetry and the other arts, and not in fiction? Between 1981 and '86, the Labour-run Greater London Council developed a funding policy supporting multi-ethnic and community arts, which was instrumental in the emergence of the influential Black Audio Film Collective, for example. Also, the newly founded public service broadcaster Channel 4 became noted for its experimental programming, facilitating wide-scale distribution of gay and working-class British films or TV shows, e.g. performance artist David Hoyle's *The Divine David Presents* and *The Divine David Heals* (1998-2000). These conditions enabled marginalised experimental forms in disciplines such as film, art and performance to emerge and, if not thrive, survive, in the UK since the 1980s. Was funding and development support available to literature in the same way, and if so, why is there no diverse legacy of British experimental fiction? In terms of racial inclusion in publishing, the Greater

Access to Publishing group (GAP) campaigned for more BAME personnel in the UK publishing workforce in the '80s, and the Arts Council initiated publishing apprenticeships at various points in the '80s, '90s and '00s. But the few BAME editors that came through had to be overly mindful that the BAME writers they commissioned (from Oxbridge, always) were commercially viable, so as not to reinforce the presumption that 'black books don't sell'.[7] Black experimental works did not fall under this category (commercial), which is, of course, another presumption ('experimental books don't sell'). The conditions of (im)possibility that prevented the emergence of BAME, LGBTQI, women's, or working-class experimental literatures in Britain historically are many-layered and under-researched. But the structures I discuss in this intro (genre, form and discipline) have something to do with it (literature's extraordinary resistance to diversification and innovation). We're back at this (classist) high and low culture thing.

iv.

Also positioned as directly opposed to literature (high culture) is subculture (it's in the name). If there is one thing we know how to do well in Britain, it's subculture. We are WORLD-LEADING at subculture. Take for example the eternally generative punk and new romantic subcultures, which channelled the defiance of a generation into off-the-scale innovation in fashion, music and radical politics in the 1980s. *New Romantic & Tender Hearts* (Waidner, *LTC*) takes as an inspiration some of the real-life 1980s DIY fashion designers, such as Sui Juris and Bodymap. To an extent, these 'small businesses' were enabled by their founders' imaginative use of Thatcher's Enterprise Allowance Scheme (a Tory initiative which gave a guaranteed weekly income to unemployed people who set up their own business). DIY designers, record labels, club promoters, etc., ended up crossing into the mainstream, partially driving the widespread public

7 Margaret Busby, 'Is it still a case of plus ca change?', in *The Bookseller*, 4 November 2016, https://www.thebookseller.com/blogs/it-still-case-plus-c-change-426096

resistance to Thatcher's government. If Zeitgeist and economic resourcefulness enabled prolific subcultural production at the time, why didn't anyone set up a DIY literary press? Or did they? Was literature part of these subcultures? Or was subcultural writing happening in zines, in 'nonliterary' formats and disciplines such as journalism (i-D, The Face)?

Precipitated by consecutive Tory governments since 2010, prohibitive rents and record levels of gentrification in London mean that the DIY spirit has gone out of fashion, literally.[8] But it's been making an entrance into publishing. Dostoyevsky Wannabe's ethos is inspired in equal measures by independent cultures that arose in the 1980s and '90s around cities as various as Glasgow, Scotland (The Pastels, Splash One), Olympia, USA (K Records, Riot Grrrl) and Dunedin, New Zealand (Flying Nun Records); and Penguin's mid-20th century philosophy of making challenging literature affordable and available to the general public. Using contemporary print-on-demand technologies, DW have developed a publishing practice that allows them to print and widely distribute their books on zero overheads and little financial capital. They are combining book publishing with design, video production (original film trailers for every books), mixtapes, a The-Face-inspired culture mag (Swimmers Club) and the DW Switchboard, a digital interface connecting writers, publishers and other subcultural producers. As part of the wider digital disruption of UK publishing (driven by journals including 3:AM, Berfrois, Gorse, Minor Literature[s] and Queen Mob's Teahouse), independent publishers like Dostoyevsky Wannabe, And Other Stories, Book Works, Dead Ink, Dodo Ink, Galley Beggar, Influx Press, or Tilted Axis are drastically changing what and whose work is being published, and as a result, what work is being written, by who. Most of the LTC contributors are lesbians, trans women, (gender)queers, some gay men. Many of us are BAME, working-class, women, migrants, or from a background of migration. We are a poster group for intersectionality by default. Intersectionality is and

8 Labels like A-Cold-Wall*, Craig Green and Nasir Mazhar have come through in London in recent years, but the clothes are expensive.

should be the norm in nonmainstream LGBTQI communities, not the exception it might be in more rarefied contexts. We are multiplicious, and so are our friends: *LTC* is edited in the spirit of inclusion and drawing alliances across differences (while being attentive to exclusions and hierarchies persisting in all of the liberation movements). Is this the emergence of a literary subculture in the UK (YES).

v. (for *v*anguard)

"This has been a sensational year for experimental fiction," *LTC* contributor Rosie Šnajdr writes in her round-up of experimental fiction in the Times Literary Supplement.[9] It has. But liberating the canon is not just a question of printing an article about work that challenges literary conventions in an institution like the TLS, nor about inserting a couple of poc or people from a working-class background in high profile editorial positions. It goes without saying that these changes are indispensable. But widening participation (to use that term) in literature also requires a critical engagement with literary form. The writing itself has to transgress the various structures through which the avant-garde literary canon has perpetuated itself and its exclusiveness. To reiterate, the writing needs to work across various systems of oppression (intersectionality), across formal distinction (prose and poetry, critical and creative, and the various genres), and across disciplines. Same goes for publishing, editing, reading, referencing and designing curricula. Change literature (or what is defined as such) and the discipline will diversify. Diversify the discipline and the literature itself will change. Liberating the canon depends on inclusion and formal innovation in equal measures. The two are interrelated.

Tasked with adding "commas and full-stops and semicolons and god-knows-what-else in the correct places" to an Eng Lang comprehension text ("it had no punctuation at all, presumably

9 Rosie Šnajdr, 'Toothsome Prose', in *Times Literary Supplement*, Nr. 5981, 15 November 2017, pp. 27-28. https://www.the-tls.co.uk/articles/private/toothsome-prose/

to prove some kind of stupid point"), Eley Williams's protagonist in *The Flood and the Keeper* escapes into "grammarless dreaming". *The Flood and the Keeper* is doing exactly the kind of literary work that needs doing now. An intently visual attempt to make sense of their own historical moment (trolls, hormones, disappointed parents), Jay Bernard's *Now I'm Nearly 30 I'm Asked For ID All The Time* is doing exactly the kind of literary work that needs doing now. (Staggering lines, literally.) Richard Brammer's *Neoliberalism* recruits Javascript to problematise supermarkets, being an autodidact not of choice but of necessity, and the reality of existing in a world not of one's making. Seabright D. Mortimer's *Supermarket Revelations* engages Luce Irigaray's critical theory in order to examine the violence of heteronormativity on a protagonist's body while shopping in Tesco (or Morrisons). All of the work included in *LTC* is doing exactly the kind of literary work that needs doing now.

Isabel Waidner, London, UK, January 2018

# JULIET
# JACQUES

## THE HOLIDAY CAMP

Sam Lightfoot was several feet taller than Snappy the Alligator, and for that reason alone, he thought he shouldn't be there. He paused, squinting at the words YOU MUST BE SHORTER THAN ME TO RIDE, watching the rain drop down Snappy's strangely forced half-smile. The go-kart track would have closed hours ago and anyone smaller than Snappy was probably in bed, and the last time he might have enjoyed a place like this was when he was little enough to race.

He entered the main building through the arcade, a few coins in his pocket. He put 10p into the penny pusher, knowing that if he thumped the glass, he'd get more money. Knowing also that this would get him thrown out, he didn't, but he won enough to play a coin-op game. Most of them were about ten years old: *Bomb Jack, Paperboy, Arkanoid,* even *Pole Position.* A few lads crowded around *Sonic Blast Man,* calling their friend a "poof" for not hitting the punch pad hard enough to smash the asteroid hurtling towards Earth.

He walked past the air hockey tables to the foyer, wondering whether his parents would have gone to the Prince Albert pub or the Casablanca Showbar. He tried the pub, where two middle-aged newlyweds were mangling *I Got You Babe* – a favourite of his mother's. He had long suspected that karaoke was the worst thing in the world and was pleased not to waste much time proving it.

He went to the bar, wondering how his parents were celebrating their final night at the camp. They were near the back with a bottle of wine and a near-empty pint of lager.

"Where's Jen?"

"She got bored," his mother replied.

"Don't blame her," said his father. "This is bloody embarrassing."

"You wanted to stay. You know I hate this kind of thing."

Sam looked at the stage. There was a drag queen in a tiara, a green dress with a skirt down to her black stilettos and a sash saying 'Helen Heigh-Water' in gold script. Her wig had blonde curls, her blue eyes had long lashes and her lipstick shined red, smudged across her face as she swigged Prosecco from the bottle.

Swaying, she finished *Big Spender.* "Seriously you posh fuckers," she yelled, "give me some money, I'm down to my last forty Benson & Hedges. Nobody's going to tell the DSS if you chuck a fiver onto the stage!" Sam was one of the few people to laugh. "What do you faggots want, hand jobs? You're not so tight that you can't part with a tenner, are you?" She drank more Prosecco and burped loudly, attracting more laughter. "We'll auction it. Five pounds for a hand job. Do I hear five pounds? No? Four fifty? Anyone?"

"I'll give you a fiver to fuck off home," yelled Sam's father. "This place has gone down the bloody pan – last year we got the Bootleg Beatles!"

"Bootleg *Beatles*, darling?" asked Helen, hitching up her skirt. "Wouldn't you prefer to stick your John in my Ringo?"

Sam's mother got up and walked out. His father downed his Stella and followed. "Yesterday, you're not half the man you used to be!" he yelled as he left, to cheers and applause.

"Oh, please say to me / You'll let me be your man / And please say to me / You'll let me suck your dick," yelled Helen, to enthusiastic laughter from Sam and boos from almost everyone else. "Ah, screw you all," said Helen, winking at Sam and then hiccupping, looking at the DJ booth. "Sweetheart, that's your bloody cue, can I have the music please?"

The bleeps and drum machine kicked in, and Helen began slurring her way through *Tainted Love* by Soft Cell. *Sometimes I feel I've got to run away, I've got to get away...*

Sam had an erection. His boxer shorts were too small; it was so sharp and painful that he raced out. "Fucking hell, love, it wasn't that bad, was it?" came from the stage, where the chorus should have been. *Touch me baby, tainted love...* He leant on Snappy, taking deep breaths to calm himself, and then walked back to the chalet. His parents had gone to bed, so he tiptoed into his room. Jen wasn't there. He wondered why she'd come – wasn't she too old for this?

Jen's suitcase was open. Sam took off his T-shirt, his jeans, his socks and his itchy boxer shorts and stood naked, gazing at the pyjamas on his pillow. He took a pair of white knickers with a lace front and put them on. Instantly, his erection sprang back.

Terrified of tearing the stitching, he tore them off. He tried a pair of pink briefs, and then pulled some black tights over them, too thin to mask his hairy legs. He grabbed a white bra, putting one strap over each arm and one sock in each cup. He couldn't fasten it and the socks fell out. "*Shit,*" he said, before worrying that he was making too much noise. He dropped the bra and put on a dress, white with a red sash. It barely covered his crotch.

He took a hairband and put it over his brown, floppy curtains. The door opened. He took it off. Too late. Jen entered and shrieked with laughter. "What the *fuck?*"

"Shush!" said Sam. "You'll wake up mum and dad!"

"What's so funny?"

Sam didn't recognise the voice. A man in a No Fear T-shirt, about 17, lanky, cropped hair, came in. "This is your brother?"

The door to his parents' room opened.

*"Quick – under the covers!"* whispered Jen, hiding him.

"What's going on in there?"

"It's fine," said Jen. "Me and Rich just woke up Sam, that's all."

The door closed. Jen prized the covers out of Sam's hands, seeing him curled up, shaking.

"It's okay, he's gone." She paused. "How long have you been doing this?"

"This is the first time, I swear."

Jen smiled. "If you don't do everything I say, I'll tell everyone in Reigate."

"And I'll tell them you've been with some guy who isn't your boyfriend."

"As if they'll believe anything you say," said Rich. "Gaylord."

"Leave him alone." Jen smiled again. "Do you like doing this?"

"No! I just –"

"I think you do," she said, tugging down his skirt and slyly brushing his leg. "Come on, let's go to the disco. Get that dress off and I'll sort out your bra." He did, and Jen put the bra over his torso, fastened it, rolled up the socks and put them back. "You'll want cotton wool next time, love. Sit still and I'll do your make-up." Sam noticed Rich glaring at him as Jen put foundation and blusher on him, then did his eyes, giving them beige shadow and long black lashes. He put the dress on and she put the hairband back, handing him a mirror.

"Feel sexy yet?"

"Yeah!"

"Great, let's go. *Quietly!* Wear these."

Jen handed Sam some black heels, a size too small. He crammed his feet into them and they left. Sam strutted across the square, looking around nervously, with Jen and Rich behind him, holding hands.

"She walks like a girl, doesn't she?" laughed Jen.

"Nice legs, too."

By the go-kart track, Sam saw the lads from the arcade, smoking. He heard whispers, laughs, and then a wolf whistle. As he got closer, they cheered. One of them blocked his path. Jen and Rich kept going, holding their ground, and the boy moved. Sam walked on, faster, pretending not to hear them yell *fucking queer.*

They went to Casablanca's, where *Blame It on the Boogie* was playing. Jen screamed, grabbed Sam's hand and yanked him to the dance floor. "Come on!" she shouted as Sam glanced at the rhythm-less forty-something couples. Rich took Jen's face and kissed her: she held him off but he pressed harder. She soon gave in, and they snuck off to a corner. Sam watched as Rich kept kissing Jen, every time she tried to get up, and although he couldn't make out what they were saying, he figured it must concern him as they kept looking at him. He started to walk over but Rick caught his eye, kissed Jen and climbed over her, so he stopped.

Having nothing else to do, Sam danced. He saw someone he thought he'd met: tall, blue eyes, jutting cheekbones, cherry lips with cropped, bleached hair, wearing an earring, tight white T-shirt and perfectly straight denim jeans. The man went to the bar and then turned to him.

*"Why did you run off?"*

"Have we met?"

"My name is Matt, but I think you know me as Helen."

"You recognise me?"

"You're the first fit boy I've seen here for years," said Matt. "Did you dress up for me?" Sam blushed and laughed. "I'll take that as a yes. It makes a nice change from the bald old fuckers and frigid trollops who usually come here."

"Those were my parents," said Sam.

"Come here, I'll teach you to dance," laughed Matt, taking Sam's hands, "as you *clearly* don't know." He led, and Sam wobbled. "This is your first time in heels, isn't it?"

Sam nodded as *Everlasting Love* hit its chorus.

"Are you alright?" asked Matt.

"People keep staring at me."

"Fuck 'em," said Matt. "Come back to the performers' chalet, there's no-one there."

Sam looked over at Rich, who was all over Jen. They didn't notice him. He took Matt's hand and they left. Matt opened the door. The sofa was covered in Helen's clothes: the dress and sash draped across it with the wig and tiara thrown over them. Heels and frocks were everywhere, interspersed with make-up and hairpieces.

"Sorry about the mess."

"I liked you better as Helen."

"You want to try it?"

Sam smiled.

"Come on," said Matt, taking off Sam's dress. "You shouldn't be wearing this Top Shop bollocks." Matt looked in Sam's bra. "Socks?"

"This *is* my first time."

"Let's make it special then. Here," said Matt, handing Sam a pair of flesh-coloured silicone breast forms, "I got these through the post."

"Where from?" asked Sam, squeezing one of them.

"Transformation. You know it?"

Sam nodded. He'd seen their adverts in the *Sunday People*, promising 'From He to She – Instantly!' but he had never spoken to anyone about it.

"Shall I put them in then?" asked Sam. Matt grabbed them and fitted them into Sam's bra, pulling up the cups when he was done.

"You want to wear the green one, don't you?"

Sam smiled. Matt unzipped it and gave it to him to step into.

Then Matt did it up and put a hairnet over Sam's head, topping it with the curly blonde wig and the tiara. He sat Sam in front of a mirror. "Lashes first, darling," he said, gluing some fake ones onto Sam's eyelids. "And now... glitter!" He smeared it across Sam's face. "Divine!" He paused, stroking Sam's shoulders, smiling at his reflection. "I'd do your lips, but..." Matt picked Sam up and kissed him. They looked into each other's eyes as Matt rubbed Sam's thigh, brushing the silk dress against his tights. Matt worked his hand up to Sam's crotch, rubbing his knickers, and then led him into the bedroom.

"You use a condom?" asked Sam.

"Always," said Matt. "So many of my friends dropped dead." He paused. "Get 'em off then."

Sam took off his underwear and laid on his front. Matt threw Sam's shirt over his back and fucked him until they both collapsed onto the bed.

"You okay?"

"It hurts."

"In a nice way?"

"Yeah."

"You'd better go," said Matt. "I don't know how old you are, and if anyone finds out then I'm in big trouble." Silence. "I'm afraid I'm going to have to ask for my tits back."

Sam laughed. He took off the dress, wig and hairnet and jutted out his chest, letting Matt take the breast forms. Matt kissed him again, handed him Jen's dress and picked up the socks.

"If you roll them up, they're more convincing," said Matt, putting them back. "And walk with your heel first."

"Thanks," said Sam.

"Keep the lashes, they suit you."

Sam left. Where was his chalet? He wandered across a few courtyards, and then remembered that Jen had the keys. Perhaps she was in? He saw their block, and their ground-floor flat. A light was on: he crept closer, cursing the noise that his shoes made on the concrete, quickly realising that he couldn't quieten it by walking over the damp grass.

Someone was in the living room. Was it Jen or his parents? The curtains were closed. He walked past the cinema, seeing that *Ace Ventura: Pet Detective* had been on. The same lads were outside, smoking. They eyed up his legs but said nothing. *Perhaps they think I'm a girl?* Sam tried to keep his head up, going for the disco. It was closed. *That must have been Jen,* he thought, *mum and dad will be in bed by now...*

He decided to avoid the cinema, taking another route back. Seeing Snappy, he felt like he'd found a friend. Then he realised that people were following him. Panicking, he stumbled in his heels, balancing himself on Snappy's snout.

*"Are you a girl or a boy?"*

"What?" said Sam, backing away as three lads cornered him against the go-kart entrance. *"ARE YOU A GIRL OR A BOY?"* Sam tried to barge through but they blocked him.

"You're a fucking geezer, aren't you?"

"Leave me alone!"

"Grab his wig!" said one, as his friend yanked at Sam's hair.

"That's real, you dick!"

"Don't call my mate a dick, you bender!"

Sam tried to run. Someone grabbed him and shoved him backwards.

"Those aren't your real tits, are they?"

He folded his arms over his chest and stood against Snappy, shaking.

*What would Helen do?*

Sam took off his heels and smacked one of the lads around the face with them. He ducked under Snappy and raced across the go-kart track, vaulting over its ridges, lifting the skirt of Jen's dress so it didn't impede his movement, and then ran to the chalet, praying that he wouldn't slip on the wet grass in his tights.

"I'll kill you!" he heard. "Faggot!"

Sam reached the chalet, desperately hoping that the door was unlocked. It was. He got inside, slammed it shut and bolted it. Struggling not to vomit, he leant on the handle, gasping for air. One of the boys banged on the door. "Get out here! Poof!" He started crying, then felt a hand on his shoulder. It was Jen.

"Are you okay? What happened?"

"Make them stop," said Sam, falling into her arms. He glanced over her shoulder at Rich, sat at the table looking at the *Daily Mail* sports section.

"Rich," said Jen, "tell them to piss off, would you?"

Rich sighed and went to the window, opening it a fraction. "Look, he's not coming out so you might as well piss off, understand?" He closed it again, glaring at the boys until they walked off. Sam made for the bedroom.

"Hold on!" said Jen. "Where have you been? We spent ages looking for you!"

"You disappeared!"

"*You* disappeared! Where did you go?"

"I was dancing with Helen."

"That rubbish drag queen?"

"She's not rubbish!"

"She?" laughed Jen. "Wait – you don't fancy her, do you? I mean *him*."

"Shut up!" whispered Sam. "I've got to go and get –"

The door to their parents' room opened. Sam's father walked out, looked at him and laughed.

"What are you doing dressed up like that?"

Sam hesitated.

"It's for a competition," said Jen.

"Which competition was that?"

"Umm... we bet Sam that he couldn't win the Miss Lovely Legs contest."

"Why the hell would you want to do that?"

Before Sam could answer, his mother walked into the living room. She shrieked. "Why are you wearing your sister's clothes?" She looked at Sam's father. "Are you just letting him do this?"

"He says it's for a competition," said his father.

"*I* didn't say that!"

They heard voices outside, giggling. Rich went to the window. "I thought I told you lot to fuck off!" The lads jeered. Sam's father walked over. "He means it – get out of here or I'll call the police!" They laughed, shouting *wanker* and *paedo* as they walked away.

"Did you win the competition then Samantha?" asked Sam's father as his mother glared at him. "Funny time to have it – in my day they were in the afternoon. And they didn't have blokes!"

"There wasn't a competition," said Sam.

"Were you copying that drag queen?" asked his mother.

"No… I just wanted to see what it felt like."

"And how does it feel?" asked Jen, before their parents could. She offered Sam a seat.

"It feels…" Sam looked at his parents, and then Jen. "It feels nice."

"Go and get changed," said Sam's father. "And don't let us see you dressed like that again."

Sam's parents went to their room. Sam went to his, closed the door and stared at himself in the mirror before taking off his clothes and trying to sleep. The next morning, after she returned from Rich's chalet and then called to say that she'd be home that afternoon, Jen gave Sam a pair of knickers. "Keep them until you can be more open," she told him. Sam put them on under his jeans and packed to leave, thinking that he would never forget the strange freedom of the camp as his parents silently drove through the exit, wondering when that time might arrive.

# ELEY
# WILLIAMS

## THE FLOOD AND THE KEEPER

It was growing late and the child was meant to be revising. They were scheduled to sit three exams the following day—*THREE*—and before any trudge upstairs to bed could be justified there were Biology articles still to read ('Multiple Choice: Adaptations in Mammals of the Savannah'), a passage about *The Impossibility of an All-Knowing, All-Powerful and All-Loving God, Question Mark* that required annotation and an Eng Lang comprehension exercise that required the child's close-enough attention.

Competition for workspace on the kitchen table-top was always fraught and this evening it involved wrestling worksheets from beneath the family's grim-faced orange cat. The child scanned the Eng Lang worksheet and its stiff little paragraph. It sat on the page with no punctuation at all. Presumably the punctuation's absence proved some kind of stupid point; the child was supposed to add commas and full-stops and semicolons and God-knows-what-else in the correct places so that the writing's meaning might be carved into easier-to-swallow pellets. The TV in the neighbouring room played something about boats overturning in the blue blue sea, and the child was so tired of it all, always all this homework to do. It was just so *arbitrary*. The child had learnt the word *arbitrary* on Friday and still getting used to practicing it in the world. They really were so tired. The orange cat tucked its head under the child's hand and, seeing an opportunity, it rolled across the papers and claimed some sort of victory.

The child pulled the heel of their hand across their eyes in an attempt to juice something like wakefulness from their brain. The text jumped a little on the page as they blinked and the cat snoozed on against the prose, the TV continued its report with a soft voice and unfathomable statistics. The child closed their eyes just for a minute. Propping their chin up on their elbows, just for a quick minute. Just for a whole minute. It is tedious to recount someone's grammarless and poorly punctuated dreams however baroque or complex they may seem to the dreamer—even though, apparently, dreams only actually occur in a split-second—but! there was a lesson to be learned here!, in this one dream!, because! this sleeping child with their sleeping face mere sleeping inches from a passage about metaphors and similes dipped into a metaphor or a simile that began with a conjunction all about enduring narratives which always prefer carpenters to zookeepers so that by the time that the child—who was now a zookeeper in their dream and finding that *they had always been a zookeeper* with zookeeper's boots and zookeeper's hands—allowed eyelid to meet eyelid this new-old zookeeper was trying to parse such terms as 'pitching timber' and 'gopher wood', '2x4s' and 'two-by-twos' passing around the nearby village by which time it was already too late for the zookeeper and their favourite animal, a creature all absurdity and grace that—*would you believe it?*—only spends between ten minutes and two hours asleep per day, so that by the end of the first week of rain in this mere-seconds dream the zookeeper's giraffe was *not* screaming at the water falling from the sky like the other animals in their enclosures but instead stood blinking half-dreams patiently in the rain and blinking at the zookeeper as they pulled on their waxed hat and their galoshes and began loosing their birds—all of which they had named, each and every one—from the cages, and loosing too the lions—which they had named, each one, arbitrarily—and also loosing the leopards, and the tiny gryphon, and the bear while the noise of the village's tin rooves-spelt-with-a-*v* or roofs-spelt-with-an-*f* grew in full percussion on account of the hail, hail that is not often mentioned in the books that describe the flood—capital-*F*—and its forty days and forty nights, since 'rain' is always the assumption, straightforward, straight-forward, but there was hail too as well as rain and sleet and even silent snow that fell snow on snow in the yard of the zoo as quietly as a giraffe that is sick to its fourth stomach, its second poor simile, its nineteenth hour of rest and its fifth questionable etymology, and—staring at the endless rain—the giraffe's tall thoughts were interrupted when the zookeeper leaned up to ask, shouting straightforwardly over the sound of water hitting stone and water hitting water, *Who will believe me that you ever existed if none of us are left?* and then the zookeeper was overcome with sentiment and they fetched a tall ladder and the giraffe waited patiently as the zookeeper climbed to its highest rung, reached out, and twiddled the ossicones on the giraffe's head, *ossicones*, the water had ruined every book in the house apart from the dictionary and the zookeeper had been looking-up and memorising giraffe-words to pass the time under the weather, *ossicones*!, the little nubs on the top of a giraffe's head, so, here, at the top of their ladder the zookeeper extended a hand and twiddled the ossicones on the top of the giraffe's head and make-believed that by doing so they could radio for help because perhaps the zookeeper was delirious, let's give them that, and they continued seething over the sound of the hail, and then soothing, and then adding, *We share the same number of vertebrae, did you know that, even with your neck so long, I read it in the funny pages* and then the zookeeper made sure that at least the sodden giraffe could have its lunch and together they tongued blossoms through acacia spininess, a treat, and every day in their split-second dream even as the waters kept rising the zookeeper took the time to brush giraffe-dust from the giraffe's coat with the longest broom in the village; last year they had constructed a shed for the express purpose of storing long brooms and the giraffe had watched them build it—happier times—but today, on the thirty-first day if we're counting, with the rain that had fallen at first in hyphens or in snow-on-snow asterisks, then falling in en-dashes, now in em-dashes, and the zookeeper watched all this through long lashes as that shed filled with brooms washed away and they saw what can happen when one overlooks definitions and ampersands and deleaturs and the zookeeper shouted apologies to the giraffe without quite understanding why, and when they were told that the waters would not stop the zookeeper began killing the animals that would not leave the yard despite being freed, killing them concertedly to spare them from drowning, and of course the zookeeper wept and swore and wept again full sore for the water of all that weeping too and as the new-tides rose the children in the villages did the same to their orange cats and yellow dogs, and a thrush did the same to some snails on a roof-top, and clouds in their bruxism eyed the mountains and set about them in a similar way, and the giraffe ruminated on the fact that even things like the incidental mice in a zoo's yard with its possessive apostrophes must scream and scream and scream at the last, but, the giraffe, in its final moments when the rain grew sharp and italic and perhaps it felt that it could not stay silent without appearing unappreciative as all flesh perished that moved upon the earth, both fowl and cattle and beast and every swarming thing that swarmeth upon the earth, as the dream-zookeeper lost the hand of their dream-wife beneath the water and while the zookeeper was coughing in the dream-water with one arm looped around the parish weathervane and saying goodbye to their giraffe, with a ship, *off there*, just glimpsable in the distance, a ship filled with clipboards and specific animals that do not really have hands so they could not wave back to the zookeeper even in misunderstanding—but for the record it looked a little like that was the case—just as this ship bobbed by, filled with pairs of animals that were somehow believed to be more worth saving, as it bobbed past and beyond the horizon and the men who decided that those animals were the ones who would be allowed to get away while others should be left behind turned their backs so to face their horizon, the zookeeper's shoulders slipped a last crucial inch and it was then that the zookeeper's favourite charge chose its moment and the tall tall tall giraffe turned its funny funny funny head against the zookeeper's cheeks and breathed across their face to keep them warm and

the child woke and forgot the dream just as the background news report ended with so much more work, grammar and paperwork still left to be completed.

# MOJISOLA
# ADEBAYO

## STARS

A play by Mojisola Adebayo with live music produced by Debo Adebayo.

### Prologue

*Voice of a Griot – West African storyteller. Projected animation film accompanies the text with music.*

Griot:
*(Calling in song)* Nommo! Nommo...!
Once, we were two,
Once two was one.
A duo in solo
The Nommo
Both female and male,
Of land and of sea,
From Po Tolo came the Nommo
Of star: Sirius B.
Beings of twin,
Fishlike-body-persons
With feet and fins,
Scales and skin,
Covered in all colours,
Desert rain chameleons...
This is a tale of tails.

The story goes:
The Nommos were
Creatures and teachers
Of the waters and the word,
Migrants 'cross the cosmos
Sailed the sky to planet Earth.
Descendants from a star that you and I cannot see –
With naked eyes at least –
Sirius B.
A galactic companion to

HuMan's best friend -
The Dog Star, the North Star
Our brightest guide in the sky
But only one part of an unseen binary
Sirius is coupled with Sirius B.

And for thousands of years,
Pre telescopic astronomy
This star was known only
To the Dogon of Mali.
Cousins to the Pharaohs?
Who knows...
They call Sirius B, 'Po Tolo'.
Po – star.
Tolo - the tiniest seed you can scatter in a field
And still grow food for your babies.
Though tiny, Po Tolo is
Very very heavy and so, so, very very light,
white...
So significant, so important, a nerve ending of the universe
Imperceptible even under the darkest sheet of the night
The whites could not see this star
Nor could the Dogon, it's too small, too far,
Yet their forefathers were told of Po Tolo
By the Nommos:
Ancestral aliens sailing to Africa in space ship from Sirius B,
Seriously.
They said it orbited Sirius every half century...

The Dogon painted all they learnt of the cosmos from the
Nommos
On the walls of their houses,
Celebrated with rituals, masks, sculptures, dances!
Dogon art was exhibited in New York-London-Paris
Making Picasso a modernist and careers for anthropologists.

And then one day through a big telescope
Old blue eyes said,

"Indeed
Sirius has a B that cannot – nakedly – be seen"
And he took a photo,
In 1970.
European scholars:
"What a wonder!
The star really is very, very, dense
Just as that remote tribe said
And it is as white as snow...
But how could these old black Africans know?
The cave paintings reveal the vastness of the universe!
Before *us* they knew of Jupiter's moons!
And the rings of Saturn – they could see!
And Sirius B does orbit Sirius for fifty years *precisely*.
They knew that the planets revolve around the sun
And that the earth was born from a big big bang,
While we were still drawing maps of the earth as flat
And believed the horizon was the end of it,
When we were still too scared to set sail,
For fear our boats would fall off into hell,
Before we stepped foot on Southern shores,
Before we were conqueristadores,
Before the birth of the three great religions
And declared ourselves civilisation's guardians,
When we still believed the sun revolved around us
And the dark creatures of the earth were wicked primitive
savages,
While we were burning witches and heretics
It seems these Africans were intergalactic!
The Dogon knew
About Sirius 'how-could-that' B...?"

"We told you,
we were told,
by the Nommos".
Extraterrestrial Afro-hermaphroditic anthro-amphibian
migrants!
Both male and female!

Of land and of sea!
Like people and fish!
With feet and fins!
Scales and skin!
Bi-beings, twins!
Rainbow chameleons!


But,
Just as Sirius B is a binary there is a companion to this story:
The Dogon believe in one God,
In the sky (sounds familiar), Amma
Who wanted the Earth as *His* celestial sexual partner
But he could not mount her
Because her 'mountain' was too big,
It got in the way,
He couldn't get it in.
The willful single mother Earth gave birth
To a jackal, a devil instead
Who Amma rejects as he could not be the father.
The jackal / devil roams around bringing the world into disorder.
So Amma created the Nommo as messengers, saviours of the world...
But even though the Nommo are
Transmitters of all the Dogon know,
They also appear troubling as doubling androgynes,
Bodies ugly and fishy with excessively fleshy differing...
So the Dogon believe to restore true social order
Brought to the world by the reckless devil-jackal son of un-mountable mother
A boy must be made to look like a boy and a girl must be made to look like a girl and we must be like Nommo, no more...


A duel of dualisms has ensued since then
Repeated the world over
In religions, traditions, medicine
Justified
With knives, razor blades and needles in hand
To make a woman a woman and a man no less a man...

This is an old tale of tails...

But once we were two
And once two was one
And some of us
Want to go home...
Nommo! Nommo!
*Music.*

## Scene – kitchen

*Mrs, an old lady dressed in black, enters her small London council flat kitchen, places an urn and her handbag on the kitchen table, where there is also a goldfish in a bowl and a newspaper. Makes a cup of tea. Takes a cigarette intently, lights it, all the while, watching the urn.*

Mrs: "What now Mrs?" *(As if quoting Mr.)* What now...
*(Mrs sits, opens The Mirror newspaper and reads her horoscope.)*
'Planetary activity in Leo including today's New Moon marks the start of a personal adventure – even at the onset of winter. Despite the fact that a pursuit of yours turned out to be 'an extended' flight of fancy, you should accept an invitation from afar, without hesitation. Keep doors open. Draw in new air. Throw caution to the wind.'
*(To the fish in the goldfish bowl.)*
Well, cat, what do we make of that?
Yes indeed, could be, could mean...
*(Mrs draws deep on her cigarette, stubs it out, then takes the packet of cigarettes and throws it into the oven and slams the door. Opens a window, takes a deep breath, coughs. Realises she is peckish. From her handbag, she takes out a triangular cucumber sandwich on white bread wrapped in a napkin. Sips her tea then eats the sandwich. Then looks at 'cat', the fish.)*
How rude. I am forgetting myself.
*(She goes to get the fish food from a cupboard. She empties the box of flakes. There are only a few flakes left. She resumes eating her sandwich.)*
Whatchu lookin at me like that? Shop's shut. *(Listens to cat, the fish.)* You'll have to wait until the morning... *(hears 'cat' suggesting*

*something, reacts shocked).* I can't do that...
You're not wrong.
*(She empties the ashes from the urn into the goldfish bowl.)*
Don't choke on it. Enjoy every minute. 'Revenge is mine sayeth the Lord.' Mr probably finished off several of your relatives, beer battered with vinegar and chips, licking his lips staggering home to manhandle his Mrs every Friday, Saturday, any day, any night. So what goes around...
*(Laughs. To the audience.)*
What must you think of me?
*(In grief for herself)* Sixty years and a day.
I was a slave.
The living dead, that was me.
He don't feel anything now do he?
He don't feel anything at all.
So nothing's changed there.
That's not a body.
There's not a God.
Only a jailer.
My sentence.
But I've served my time in this space.
I've known my place.
What now?
*(A door-bell rings. Projection of visuals through a spy hole.)*


Later...


Scene – Mrs and Mary become friends


*Mrs is at the door, looking brighter, smoking a vape. A girl, around 11 years old, East African accent, is at the door.*


Mrs: Hello again little friend.
Girl: I brought you these, for my birthday *(hands a box of chocolates - Celebrations).*
Mrs: But it's not my birthday.
Girl: I know, that's why I said it, my birthday.
Mrs: Oh, happy birthday. Aren't you the one supposed to be

getting presents?

Girl: I got lots of presents. I got Barbie, I got new dress, I got... a holiday.

Mrs: Oh... going anywhere nice?

Girl: Been already.

Mrs: Oh good, I mean...

Girl: Came back for big school starting. I saved Celebrations. Mum said I should, to say thank you, for yesterday's toilet.

Mrs: Oh right. Well. I shouldn't really but... Come in then.

*(Mrs goes over to the table with the girl. She is scared of the fish.)*

Mrs: He's all right, he don't bite. If my furry friend Fina was still alive she'd likely have scratch but this cat's safe in his bowl.

*(Girl looks confused.)*

Mrs: What's your favourite?

Girl: Number 3 Galaxy, Number 2 Milky Way, Number 1 Mars. I love planets and stars. I'm going do a project. For school. I am going to win the prize. I am going be a space woman.

Mrs: Oooh a little Lieutenant Uhura. I always felt a bit like her all those years at British Telecom after my son came along. "Hailing frequencies open Captain."

Girl: What?

Mrs: Star Trek.

Girl: No, Star Trek is not real. I am going to be real, like Mae Jaemison.

Mrs: Who?

Girl: First black woman to go up. But I am going to be the first from my country. *(She points up.)*

Mrs: "Phone home..."

Girl: Huh?

Mrs: ET.

Girl: I don't know what you are talking about.

Mrs: Well evidently you have got a lot to learn about outer-space.

Girl: I know. I need more science. September. I am going to study hard.

Mrs: Right. Well you better have a Mars then. I'll put the kettle on.

*(To the audience.)*

Mrs: And that's how it began. She'd have a fifteen-minute pee

and I'd have a Celebration with a vape and a cup of tea.
"What are you doing in there Mary...?"
She said she liked the quiet
She said she liked my toilet
The knitted loo-roll holder and 'Ideal Home' magazines from the 80s...
Feeling sorry for the grieving old lady
She'd buy me *The Mirror*, daily
Girl: But *The Metro* is free?
Mrs: Sometimes you gotta pay for quality Mary.
Her name wasn't even Mary
Her name was Maryam
But no one at school could say it right
And Mary sounded less Muslim
She went to Catholic school see
The primary attached to my parish
And after that British soldier got his head chopped off in Woolwich
It was easier to be a Mary than a Maryam

*Hail Mary full of grace*
*Blessed art thee amongst women*
*And blessed is the fruit of thy womb, Jesus*

I became an evangelist for ten minutes
Searching for "the final frontier", a way, away...
Got born again
Bathed in the blood of the lamb
Bit of a phase when Mr was having another affair
I was lonely... and you got free chicken on a Sunday
But Venus must have had enough of his drinking n' pissing in the bed so he came back and shat in ours instead
And I went back to being a Catholic.
God help me.
Maybe I needed a reason to stay with him, maybe I needed to know leaving was a sin. Maybe I was scared of... freedom.
And being Catholic is much more straight-forward than being a happy clappy. You know where you stand when in Rome.

I could just never fall in the
Evangelical hall,
I have never been very good at being ecstatic.
I looked around one revival
And it was like they were all having seizures,
A room full of trembles and fits,
Mouths open, heaving breathing,
Flaying around and all talking in tongues
Sounding like
"Mymmmmamamazgottasuzukimypapasgottahondamyppppapa
sazgottasuzukimamamassgottahonda..."
But I didn't go nowhere,
I just stood there
Facing the preacher
Conducting all this energy
But no matter how hard he pushed my head
I just couldn't let go of my bones.
I just stood there on my own two feet
He ordered me, "sit down", instead
So I prayed
Cross legged
And when it was all over I had chips and curry sauce on the bus
home.
My kind of communion.
Chris would always wait for me to leave the service
Pretend he was going the same way,
He was one of those hippy holys
Long black hair like Samson but
Apparently harmless.
The Lord got him off heroin, Church was full of people with
addictions
Chris got me talking on the 181 about unlikely attractions
How he "liked older women and there was nothing against it in
The Bible, Old Testament or New"...
And as I dunked my chips in the curry sauce I confessed to him
that I had once loved a woman and my husband was my biggest
regret.

He went silent.

I didn't realize it was me Chris had a crush on.

Not very Christ like

I was fifty-fucking-seven, he could have been my son.

How I missed my son... but he said he couldn't bear to see me with the old man, so he went off spinning with his discs across the world...

Chris on the other hand was half the man of my son.

Prick went and told someone who was giving him spiritual counseling

That he had an obsession for some kind of... *(whisper)* lesbian.

Of course it went around the congregation like a house fire.

They hauled me in to a house meeting

In the middle of the week,

Told me "that is why the holy-ghost cannot enter your house",

"Your body is a temple and you haven't kept it clean",

"That is why your husband treats you the way he did",

"That's why he turns to other women and drink",

Even said that was why I had that "last miscarriage",

Even without a kick in the stomach from Mr,

Even though he hadn't thrown me against the wall – that time,

Even though he carried the laundry basket for six months like it was something to write home about,

They said my sin

Was why I

Lost my Gabrielle,

My wingless angel,

who I loved even if she was disabled,

Who I loved even though Mr said she was better off dead.

The bastard.

They said that's why "you are not able to laugh, be slain in the spirit, speak in tongues..."

Said "Satan has a hold",

Said "your womb has an omen",

Tried to pray the "demon of lesbianism out" of me,

Said it entered in through "horoscopes, sci-fi films and pagans in my ancestry".

They brought out a saucepan

LeCreuset no less
A big heavy orange one
Very middle class
All placed their white hands on my black curly head and pressed.
I leant over the pan,
They expected the demon to come out in vomit
But all I could manage was a little bit of spit.
Always such a disappointment.
Never felt right with the evangelicals after that
And then when that Freddie Mercury from Queen died
And the preacher said he got what he deserved, AIDS, the curse,
I thought, none of this sounds like Jesus or mother Mary to me
And I loved *Bohemian Rhapsody*,
Now that could take you to outer space...

*Music and visuals.*

Scene - Mary and Mrs observe

Mary changed my night to day. She worked on her project every
day until 6 and learnt her lessons by teaching me.
My flat became an observatory.
We're watching the whole constellation of the council estate
from my kitchen window.
We sit side by side and survey the 'neighbouring planets' over the
dishes in the sink. She talks me through it all while I have a vape.
'The universe accelerates,' she said.
Well it looks like our estate is going backwards...

Scene - conversation after watching the neighbouring planets /
neighbours:

Mrs: Who am I then?
Girl: Earth.
Mrs: Me? Earth? No.
Girl: Yes. You are.
Mrs: Why?
Girl: Because, I like you but you are mostly blue and covered in

clouds.

Mrs: Oh.

Girl: And Mr, he is like moon, always following you around, even though he is dead.

Mrs: Bloody hell.

Girl: And Mrs you are not healthy *(pointing to the vape)*. This is not good for you. I read it in *Metro*.

Mrs: Heavens. Anything else?

Girl: No.

Mrs: Quite finished?

Girl: Yes.

Mrs: Well thanks very much for the advice little Miss Einstein.

*(Silence.)*

Mrs: I'm not exactly mother earth then.

Girl: Sorry.

Mrs: It's all right. You're probably right. I never even knew how to grow a tomato from my balcony. It was always an ashtray, an escape... But you little one are the sun, brightening up my day.

*(Mary smiles.)*

Scene – revelation

She said "it burnt, hotter than the sun."

Like no temperature you would touch.

"When I was cut... in the Summer holidays."

"My eyes" clenched shut.

Little fists.

"They pinned me down.

Hands pressing on my shoulders, legs, head...

It was so painful."

Shameful. How could they?

But she insisted "they did it because they love me."

Her parents.

That's why she wouldn't let me phone social services.

"They might take me away! Please Mrs, don't say..."

And I know it's selfish but

I didn't want to tell no one neither.

I was afraid they might take her from me too...

So "it's our own little secret."
Why she liked to use my toilet.
Why it took her 15 minutes to pee.
Why it "stung" and she sobbed and "transported" herself "to the stars"
Why she needed to confide in me
Why some days she was in "agony".
Why she shuffled her feet across the estate
Why she was loosing weight.
No matter how many galaxies she ate.
She said:
"When you look into the stars you look into the past...
But you can't change it."
But if I could, I would...
*Holy Mary, Mother of God*
*Pray for us sinners now and in the hour of our death...*

## Scene - Why?

Mrs: Why? Mary, Maryam why...?
Girl: Tradition.
Mrs: Yes but why?
Tradition.

Later she said:
Girl: Mrs I asked my mum, about that thing.
Mrs: Did you? What did she say?
Girl: She said it is special thing, this tradition, she said English people don't understand and I should never talk about it. I'm not talking about it, OK Mrs?
Mrs: OK.
Girl: She said it happened to my brother too, when he was 13, but I was braver than him, I was younger too, I got presents, more than my brother I got a new dress!
Mrs: That's different Mary, what they cut off the boys ain't the same.
Girl: It's not true. My mum said, little girls have a bit, little boys have a bit, both gets cut, because if we didn't, I would grow into a

boy and he would grow into a girl and where we would be then? No one would know who is who.

Mrs: It don't grow into a willy Mary...

Girl: And then I asked why after they cut me they close me, why they tie my legs, why they sew me up, why I cannot pee why it hurt so much mum? She said it happen to her too, and to my grandmother and to everyone woman I know in my family since the beginning. She say it makes us all clean. She says it will keep me calm. They seal me up to keep me pure, beautiful virgin for marriage.

Mrs: Mary it's not the same.

Girl: But my mum said!

Mrs: Mary what you got, what you *had*, down there, is supposed to feel nice and no one is supposed to touch it unless you want them to, and when they do it is supposed to feel like the best thing in the whole world.

Girl: What is the best thing in the whole world?

Mrs: I dunno. Ice cream. It's supposed to feel like ice cream in the sunshine down there. It won't make much difference to your brother Mary, except he'll probably never get his winkle caught in his own zipper.

Girl: I don't understand.

Mrs: Neither do I.

girl: It is supposed to feel nice? It just hurts Mrs, all the time, it just hurts...

*(Pause.)*

Girl: You feel nice? With Mr?

Mrs: You can't ask me that!

Girl: Why you ask me questions then?! I am not a girl any more Mrs. I know things now.

*(Pause. Breath.)*

Mrs: I don't feel nothing, he's dead.

Girl: No before he went to heaven...? What was it like, on your wedding night?

Mrs: He's not in heaven Mary, there's not a hell big enough for him and it was never like ice cream. But me an you dear, its not the same.

Girl: Why?

Mrs: Because you're just a child and I've had a chance. I'm an old girl. I'm a soft old bourbon in the bottom of the tin. I've had my chances you ain't!

Girl: You're making me sad! I have chances, lots of them. I am going to be a space woman. My mum and dad they love me. I am going to bring them back a rock from the moon. They're not like you and Mr! This is our culture. They said now I am cut every man will want me. If I didn't no one would want me. And what will happen to me after they are gone if no one will want me in this far away country. They love me... It's just... Owwwwwwww... I have to pee.

Mrs: She shoved past me and then left straight after that. Didn't even stay for chocolate or a chat. Not even to work on her project. She came back the next day but wouldn't cross my doorstep. She was holding a Barbie doll in a pink dress. She thrust it into my face.

Girl: Look!

Mrs: That's nice. Your birthday present?

Girl: Look! Underneath look.

Mrs: What is it Mary?

Girl: Nothing. Nothing there. Just like me. I am pretty.

Mrs: You are pretty Mary.

And then she cried, and held her stomach.

You want to come inside? You want to pee?

Girl: NO! Mum says I cannot come any more. Mum says your husband didn't love you, because you are not clean. And he died. And now no one comes to visit, not even your son, somewhere playing music so he can be far away. In my country everyone is together. Under one sky. Only war can tears us apart. I am cut but you are cut too. And covered in scars. But I am going to be a space woman, the first woman from my country and I don't need this dirty thing. Mum and Dad will provide me everything. And when I am grown up I will provide them. You don't have any body. You want me to be your child but I am not yours. You don't even have any dreams, just TV reality, a cigarette that is not a cigarette and a cat that is really a fish. And she started to cry and she started to pee and she shuffled away, across the estate.

Mrs: Mary come back! Come in and - what about your project

Mary? Maryam?!
She didn't look back.
I watched out from my window after school but I couldn't see her for days. I knocked on their door but it seemed as if they'd gone away. And then I dreamt there was an eclipse of the sun.

Scene – eclipse

The cold moon passes in front of the sun.
We all stand in the middle of the estate with cardboard glasses on.
All the neighbours look up at the sky, together.
But I am looking at the neighbours.
Some cry, some cheer, some are filled with fear.
The birds fall silent.
And we all feel bitterly cold.
And when I get home,
There's a fish floating in a bowl and I know...
Gravity is a grave, she'd say... It can only go one way... No matter how hard we pray...

I could never go back to church after that. Even Catholic. I had no stomach for praying to a virgin. I had no stomach for tradition, religion, I had no stomach for any of it. I want to go to the stars for Mary. I want to go to the stars because she can't. And that's how it started.

*End of extract.*


ABOUT

*STARS* is a new play with animation and music that tells the story of an old lady who travels into outer space... in search of her own orgasm. The play poetically explores the power and politics of pleasure for women, girls and intersex people. It questions why millions of people are prevented from being able to reach the heights of sexual pleasure as a result of sexual trauma and genital mutilation practices, traditions and surgical interventions that continue to this day, on every continent and connects all these themes with space travel. Here are some extracts from *STARS,* to be produced and published in full in London, 2018. See www.mojisolaadebayo.com for details. *Mojisola Adebayo: Plays One* is available from Oberon Books.

Thank you to Nicole Wolf, Kameradin of my dreams, thanks to my brother and collaborator on *STARS* Debo Adebayo and last but not least big thanks to Rachel Anderson and Cis O'Boyle of idle women who's residency on board Selina Cooper in 2016 enabled me to research these themes.

# ISABEL
# WAIDNER

## FANTÔMAS TAKES SUTTON

A character called Fantômas wouldn't work. Coming from a 42-year-old writer, and a lesbian at that. Calling a character Fantômas would be infantile, also ill-advised. The self-infantilisation of the butch lesbian is proverbial as it is. (Picture a bale of butches watching a rerun of *Back to the Future*.) It's bad enough that I have the appearance of a boy cusping the age of consent (from afar). I pass as a boy or a young man in Sutton. Only yesterday, I accessorised my rolled up carrot leg type of trousers with orange socks. I came in for suburban abuse (verbal, poof). I might boycott boy fictions like *Fantômas*. Between 1911 and 1913, 32 *Fantômas* classic volumes were published in France. I have not read them. Not one. Amazon lists 24 available copies of *The Daughter of Fantômas* alone. Allain & Souvestre, the original authors, wrote this (an excerpt):

"Fantômas."

"What did you say?"

"I said: Fantômas."

"And what does that mean?" (1911, p. 1)

I don't know. I don't know what that means. Of 32 classic volumes I have yet to read one.

Reading or not reading *Fantômas* is not a question of age, nor gender. If reading *Fantômas* were a question of gender (which it is not), I would be your man. I have listened to the self-titled debut LP of the American avant-metal supergroup Fantômas. Fantômas are vocalist Mike Patton (Faith No More, Mr. Bungle), drummer Dave Lombardo (Slayer), guitarist Buzz Osborne (Melvins) and bassist Trevor Dunn (Tomahawk). Fantômas are testosterone-fuelled. Having listened to *Fantômas* the LP in the past, I no longer listen to it in the present. I have learnt not to invest in obsolete forms of masculinity such as those reproduced in the avant-metal genre and subculture. Quentin Crisp, Moj of the Antarctic, Patricia 'Bunny' O'Rooley, Peggy Shaw, Campbell X, The Divine David, Le Gateau Chocolat and Lisa Blackman, as gender nonconforming role models, outperform Fantômas's band members hands down. In many respects, Sutton outperforms America hands down. Quentin Crisp grew up in

Sutton. I finished my novel *Gaudy Bauble* in Sutton. After two consecutive Tory governments, I am no longer in a position to live in London. I live in Sutton now.

During the 1960s, various Italo-Latin publishing franchises reconfigured the French fictional character Fantômas as a Marxist superhero with homoerotic appeal. One issue of a Mexican series included a Julio-Cortázar-like persona that "so amused the author (Julio Cortázar) that he produced a meta-text/ pamphlet utilizing the comic's illustrations and plot structure" (2014, Frieze 166). In 2014, Cortázar's pamphlet, titled *Fantômas contra los vampiros multinacionales* (1975), was newly translated and republished by the US publisher Semiotext(e). As concerns Cortázar personally, he was rumoured to have been a closeted gay or closeted bisexual. Further, he was rumoured to have died from AIDS on February 12th, 1984, foreshadowing my 10th birthday on the 14th. If only Julio Cortázar were alive today, he might identify as transgender, nonbinary, or gender nonconforming (preferred pronouns: she and her). She might migrate to Sutton. She might assimilate culturally, acquire a British passport, a weird sense of humour, a limp wrist and trans feminist politics. Julio and I might get together and inaugurate a global renaissance of postmodernist fiction and, crucially, the advent of a queer avant-garde. *Si c'était Fantômas?* (1933) the people of Sutton might ask. (Sporadically, we might appear in public.) Mais non! C'était Waidner & Cortázar, international migrants. Purchasing wild clementines in Morrisons, Sutton, and a pack of spaghetti. They share a foreign publisher, the people of Sutton might say, Semiotext(e). Only yesterday, Semiotext(e) requested an excerpt from *Gaudy Bauble* for their occasional intellectual magazine, *Animal Shelter.*

Mostly I am resigned to the death of Julio Cortázar, his closeted life and his binary gender identity. I am resigned to the marginalisation of postmodernist fictions and the predominance of conceptual forms of writing in experimental literature contexts in 2018. I am resigned to my personal incompatibility with Fantômas 1 & Fantômas 2, the classic French villain and the US avant-metal supergroup. But I am invested in Fantômas 3. *Fantômas contra los vampiros multinacionales* takes as its theme the destruction of books, literature, libraries and, ultimately, humanity itself. Already libraries are decimated in Tory Britain and global humanity is teetering on the brink. Only yesterday, I wore an oversized Philip Treacy trilby and I coded 'poof' in Sutton. I am resigned to that, too. But Fantômas 3, a homoerotic, socialist superheroine, remains top of my suburban agenda.

## AVANT-ICE

If I had a superpower, I would be an ice skater. I would be a genderqueer figure skater, skating eights, loops, and axels, the whole s/hebang.

An axel is a figure skating jump with a forward take off. An Ina Bauer is an element in which the skater glides on two parallel blades. Moves in the field (MIF) is the name given to elements that emphasise basic skating skills and edge control. I am better rehearsed at controlling my edge than your average figure skater (I have an edge to me). Having controlled my edge for so long, I am MIFfed at my failure to purchase a competition dress through the obvious channels.

Competition dresses cost £35 on eBay, I checked yesterday. A custom-made leotard costs just £12. Sellers are so keen to sell their ice skating gear, they offer free postage and packaging. One seller is offering to *pay* potential takers in return for collecting her ice skating crap. Despite this glut in the second-hand market, the competition dresses on eBay are not for me. They do not have my name on it (Dean). Invariably, they are for persons aged 5 to 14. I'm 42. You might call it an equal ops issue. Structural ageism is blighting the sports of figure skating.

Personally, I came late to the sports. I did not come to figure skating until I was in my thirties. When I was a child, I did not know the first thing about figure skating. I had not heard of Torvill and Dean, nor their gold medal winning performance at the 1984 Sarajevo Winter Olympics. My parents had a TV in '84, but I did not watch the performance. Figure skating did not appeal to me. I was a butch child. Figure skating was sissy. Age 10, I adopted the butchest name I could think of (Torvill). Hi Torvill, my friends would say. Do you want to celebrate your Geburtstag (birthday) at the Eistreff Waldbronn? Skates for hire, 2 Mark per hour? No thanks, I replied. I was so polite. I will not hire women's or girls' skates for 2 Mark per hour. Nor will I be given the eye by the skate hire attendant for hiring boys' skates. I will not be referred to as Schwuchtel (faggot), λεσβία (dyke), or andersrum (queer), by amateur ice skaters and their amateur parents. Not in this European backwater I won't, not in 1984. Despite the contemporary popularity of androgynous subcultures in the UK (New Romanticism, New Wave, think Billy Mckenzie, Annabella Lwin, or Poly Styrene), androgyny never hit rural Waldbronn. Androgyny did not figure in rural Waldbronn, rendering the hiring of ice skating boots a catch-22 situation for a 10-year-old butch. You go, I said to my friends. Have fun. Age 10, I rejected ice skating for life. The rhinestoned femininity of the female skater and her gendered skates ran counter to my budding butch industry.

I have come to figure skating only recently, in connection with my ongoing transition. Having changed my name from (butch) Torvill to (masculine) Dean, I have turned increasingly girly and figure skatey. As middle-aged Dean, I have taken to ice like a duck to water. One life event in particular worked as a catalyst for my identity U-turn, my half-pirouette in regards to figure skating.

On 11th July 2000, anti-drag artiste David Hoyle marked the end of his short-lived television career with a one-off live performance at Streatham Ice Rink, entitled The Divine David On Ice. According to the flyers that were circulating at the time, Hoyle and his collaborator were to reinvent themselves as the post-gay post-modern Torville [sic] and Dean for the millennium. A flyer was a pre-internet advertising device intended for public distribution. Event promoters tended to produce flyers as part of an inexpensive and purpose-orientated grassroots practice. Flyers were not about the tactility of real paper, nor the smell of actual print. Flyers were about inclining a community that way inclined to attend The Divine David On Ice at Streatham Ice Rink, SW16.

Giving cold shoulder to fags trying to cruise me (by mistake), I witnessed Hoyle and his collaborator revolutionise modern ice dance. No video recordings exist of the event, but performance studies scholar Dominic Johnson documented Hoyle's oral account in An Oral History of Performance Art (2005). What I remember about The Divine David On Ice is that the Death March was played on a xylophone, gradually turning into Hello Dolly. The show was pandemonium on ice, not to mention the rear stalls. Nobody attending was particularly youthful or young.

Name any of David Hoyle's subsequent shows and I will vouch for the fact that none of his audiences were ever particularly youthful or young.

My problem with child size competition skates is that I prefer my footwear extra large. Wearing oversize footwear is a dykey thing and a gender subversion strategy. Only yesterday, I searched eBay for a rhinestone affair in an adult size 8. I found nothing. I resorted to purchasing second-hand ice hockey skates, stick-on diamantes, a new pair of tracksuit bottoms and eye-shadow from Rimmel. Et voilà, my competition dress was complete.

Every day, we, there are many of us, are practising MIFs, Ina Bauers and axels at Streatham Ice Rink, not under the scrutiny of our parents or coaches, but met with the indifference of the ice rink's members of staff. No one cares whether or not we're improving. No one is championing us. But I like to think of us as an avant-garde ice skating movement, acquiring momentum. Rehearsing nontraditional capabilities, DIY styles and transgressive methods, we are reforming our discipline from the margins. Committed to an Olympic-level training regimen, I lace up my hand-me-down ice hockey skates and enter the glistening arena.

## NEW ROMANTIC & TENDER HEARTS

I used to manufacture jewellery incorporating Fray Bentos tins at the heart. This was New Romantic designer fashion, at its heart was not normally processed meat. Wearing top-to-toe House of Sui Juris or Bodymap outfits, my amateur models would carry their respective Fray Bentos jewels close to their hearts. Fray Bentos necklaces were energising cardiac regions en masse in '84, and arguably the radical Zeitgeist that distinguished the period. This was the height of New Romanticism, at the heart of its industry was not normally processed meat. A resourceful use of Margaret Thatcher's Enterprise Allowance Scheme (which provided a weekly income to unemployed people who set up their own business)? *That* was at the heart of its industry.

It is true that faggots were at the heart of New Romanticism. Girl faggots, boy faggots, fags of all genders. Faggots are a processed meat and traditionally made from pig's heart, entrails and offal. Processing tenderises the heart (the entrails, offal). The heart is not deceitful but tough above all things. My Fray Bentos jewels contained in one body both denotations of the homonym faggot, at one remove. Via processed meat, Fray Bentos signified faggot signified homo. That's what the '80s and '90s were like, brimming with subversive subtexts. This was a queer semiotics, dragged down to the level of DIY jewellery. The heart is not only tough but tender above all things. Offal is literally "off fall", what falls off a butchered carcass. Owing to my personal tenderheart, I have yet fully to process Rainer Werner Fassbinder's *In a Year of 13 Moons* (1978), the West German drama film. One of the key scenes takes place in an abattoir. The scene features carcasses, entrails, offal, ad infinitum. I watched the VHS alone in a red-wine-soaked kitchen in Primrose Hill in '04. Compared to the '80s, the '00s were a very different time.

Fassbinder's film recounts Elvira, formerly Erwin, Weishaupt's final days leading up to her suicide. Elvira had "the op" (top and bottom) to assuage an abusive boyfriend, Anton, who felt offended by Erwin's effeminacy. Anton might really love Erwin if he, Erwin, were actually female. Es ginge höchstens, wenn du eine Tussi wärst. Faced with post-op Elvira, Anton leaves her regardless. Homophobia, denial, transphobia and misogyny were rife in Frankfurt am Main in '78, whereas I have the feeling that my left-leaning social media today are rifer, rifest, with diverse forms of misogyny. Over the course of *In a Year of 13 Moons*, Elvira revisits scenes from the past that were instrumental to her disintegration. The abattoir is Elvira's former workplace and first site of trauma (closeted Erwin once was a butcher's apprentice and the fiancé of the butcher's daughter). An abattoir is a meat processing plant, and as such, at the heart of faggottery. Fagottery is what landed me here in the first place. Elvira! I call, stepping out from behind a carcass hung from a butcher's hook. Elvira, hello! I'm wearing not one, not two, but three of my Fray Bentos necklaces, for good luck. I'm wearing Gosha tracksuit bottoms, an A–Cold–Wall★ T-shirt, and Reebok hi-tops in Frankfurt am Main, '78. Hi Isabelo, Elvira whispers. Elvira is so depressed in her abattoir. She is wearing a floppy felt hat, a veil of black lace, red lipstick and black stilettos. Let's go, Elvira, I say. Let's get out of here. This meat processing plant is so unwelcoming. Elvira agrees.

As part of her urge to retrace the events that were instrumental to her disintegration (and in close adherence to Fassbinder's script), Elvira insists we visit the convent and orphanage she used to inhabit as a boy. Monks, nuns and social workers were always abusing orphan Erwin within an inch of his life. Elvira intends to confront her ghosts, look them straight in the eye. I agree on the condition that we confront my own very similar ghosts, too. Mine first, Elvira demands. She drives a powerful bargain. Elvira and I are bickering outside the convent when oh hello! Who are you? What brings you here? At this juncture (debating outside the convent), Elvira and I are joined by Jillian Holtzmann, (one of) the lesbian protagonist(s) from *Ghostbusters*, the supernatural comedy film. Holtzmann is in love with Elvira and my ghostbusting sensibilities and strong girlboyish looks. She implores us to let her fight our respective ghosts with us. We say yes ok. Holtzmann does not think that looking them straight in the eye is the best way to bust ghosts. You're the expert, I say. Elvira and Isabelo, Holtzmann continues, let's really hurt our respective ghosts (since I, too, have visitations). You, Holtzmann?

You, too?! Above and beyond dealing with the psychological haunting, Holtzmann suggests we prosecute our historical perpetrators in real life. Ok, let's involve the law and the police, can we trust them. No. Not yet. In the (trans)feminist future we might. Then what, Holtzmann? What now? Let's do it ourselves. OK, pow! Take that, Elvira's ghosts. Pow pow, and that, Isabelo's ghosts. Watch out, Jillian's ghosts! We are busting you in real life.

Watching the VHS alone in a council flat kitchen in Primrose Hill, I was psychologically ill-equipped for Fassbinder's *In a Year of 13 Moons*. I was too young to process its impact in '04, just as I had been too young for New Romanticism in '84. I was 10 in '84. I was not really vending Fray Bentos jewellery at the Great Gear Market, Hyper Hyper, nor anywhere near the King's Road or World's End, West London. I was in Frankfurt am Main in '84, too young for most things that happened to me. My foray into fashion design did not occur until '94, when I was forever sewing the *Ghostbusters* logo onto second-hand sweatshirts in a warehouse in Shoreditch. i-D Magazine was peddling an aesthetic at the time that might be considered a commodification of the New Romantic DIY ethos. I did not upscale my production into a meaningful industry in '94. But in 2018, Elvira Weishaupt, Jillian Holtzmann and I are wearing Fray Bentos necklaces as tokens of faggottery, fortifying our tenderhearts and ghostbusting stamina.

## ABOUT

Versions of *Fantômas Takes Sutton*, *Avant-Ice* and *New Romantic & Tender Hearts* were first published in 3:AM Magazine (eds. Joanna Walsh & Eley Williams), Minor Literature[s] (eds. Eli Lee & Fernando Sdrigotti) and Berfrois (ed. Russell Bennetts). Thanks to the editors. Special thanks to Lisa Blackman.

# ROSIE
# ŠNAJDR

## BINGO THE DRUNKMAN

In arrears: ear-rent for knight errant. Errant night rent by Drunkman erring. Errorprone. Drunkman's speech wound. Wound round in inner ear. Intertia-reels whirring. Errand of mercy me. Mercy me. O Drunkman I hate you get up

*Errata.*

1. Drunkman mercy me. Legitimate object of objection. I am, not he. Unwounding the capacity to wound; avowing the wounds legitimacy. Gendering the wounds legitimacy. I am not he.

2. Drunkman mercy brokes no he-he. No he-he him. Ok, once. Once there was hoo-hoo. A he-he he hoo-hoo. Whopper whorling whoring hoo-hoo. No homo but. No homo but homo butt once. A reel man can slip. A reel man schtick sticking in inertia-reels. A real man can-can. Drunkman can broke no he-he.

3. Marry her. Marry her. Why won't you? Marry her. You can, you know. It's fine. I will buy. I will buy you. A drink. No thank you, Drunkman. I hate you get up

4. Drunkman have many ho-ho friend. Homofiend. Homofend. Homofiller. Homofont. A, he-he, hoo-hoo friend. A teen girl screen girl on lustrate. A teen girl screen girl good-friend-time. A her-her. With purple hair. You know her? No? So much incommon, incommoning, incoming, so much in common in coming. Tell me what you do in bed?

5. How do you do? How do you do it? The he-he do in the do-do. Said that did I that I did that once? Once. No homo. How do you do? How do you hoo-hoo do though? How do hoo hoo do the do? Wandering whets the point.

6. The errorman, reels whereing to stimulus us. A semi- semi- semi- seminal premise. Here is the curé. see? A curette to malt our bitter. A wand-waving paster-man's seminary promise. Teach

us a lesson. A bit of who's your father's all you need. A bit of how's father to turn us rite. To turn again. To turn and not turn. Teach us to sit still. That ternary premise—a bit of. Fool. A bit of. Fool. A bit of how's. Fool—the fool's how.

# STEVEN J. FOWLER

## THE BASSMENT GALLERY

"And yet this drowning in space was accompanied by an extraordinary rise of the concrete, we were in the cosmos, but as though we were in something terrifyingly definite, determined in every detail." Witold Gombrowicz. *Pornografia*

I could see him trying to lie still, as though the pain would leave him should he manage to be completely unmoving. For a moment he seemed to find this relief, his face masked in a pulsing heat over the hard, unrelenting suffering that had inflicted him moments before. But then he moved again, not so it would just down to his bodies shock, the quivering aftermath of what he had suffered but at a memory, something flashed across his face as he recalled something. I looked up, above him, nothing but a plain wooden ceiling. Panelled over concrete. He was remembering the implements perhaps, or the narrative of the work they had done to him. He was making it real in his mind, describing to himself the shape, length and colour of the instruments, where on his leg they had begun, where they had pierced the skin and the direction they had begun to sew. So his body moved, voluntarily, and in so doing the scabs on his arms, which I assume must also cover his back, became irritated, breaking into little wet red patches that made them appear from a distance like bacteria multiplying under a microscope. I saw some of the fluids was more yellowish, or made so against his skin, perhaps translucent. Not burns though, each wound was intended in its shape, small crosses or straight lines. I could see the burns on his hands, around his knuckles and fingers, still dusted with ash.

There were four beds in an otherwise empty chamber. Each bed was occupied. Each occupation was covered in a white gown that laid upon them like a sheet. The colouring of the sheet, from left to right, descended from bright and clean to almost entirely pink. Each occupant was bound with strong straps fashioned around their hands, feet and neck. While the body on the left could strain against those binds, the one on the furthest right seemed stuck to them, healed into the leather. It was the centre right body that I had first become fixed on. I was sure on the far right I could pieces of metal on the skin, or in it.

They lay utterly without a sound. The silence somehow resembled relief, as though the four occupants were grateful. Perhaps just not to be being wounded at this moment. I looked for the source of light in the room but could not see one. Not on the walls nor on the ceiling there was fixed a lamp, and yet the light was even throughout the room, not the corners, nor the beds, nor the roof was lit any more or less than the other. The colours, besides the colours of flesh, were indiscernible, blue perhaps, or a dirt green. Or grey. On ocean colour, a bad weather colour. As my eyes acclimatised so I could make out the smallest movement on the body to the furthest right, the movement of eyes in their sockets. But even more pronounced was this rapid, darting motion because it was framed so tightly, as the sockets had clearly been suffered massive damage and had puffed up into black, grazed bruises. I felt a sudden shock of illness, and the clear though that the wounds to this bodies eyes itched. Each glance, it seemed, to the others, to the walls, brought a twinge of pain that lasted because it could be expressed, or at all escaped.

The first two occupants on the left had their eyes tightly shut, as if they had had them previously pried open, and literally so, both having purple lesions on their foreheads and upper cheeks. They closed them tightly, as though they might go blind otherwise. It occurred to me then that perhaps the third and fourth occupants had indeed been blinded, and that the rapid, desperate glances of those in the latter beds were the looks of sight lost, of looking for something in the dark. The third body seemed braced against something, squinting, as though it had seen flashes coming, or a vehicle driving for it. These were small, nurtured movements, attempted while trying not to break the cuts that laced its exposed legs and arms and face. Suddens explosions of light were hitting their eyes, my eyelids themselves seemed to burn and I rubbed them involuntarily.

I saw then, taking in these finer details, how they had been brought into states of despair in order, in careful hierarchy. Was this to measure the severity of their crimes? Or about the passage of time? Would each see what was to befall them as it happened?

Would each know the worst of all, their determined fate? Until then the fourth bed, and the great relief of knowing you were soon to drop off the conveyor. Unless there was another gallery?

A convulsion from the first body, its every move, despite the relative lack of blood outside the skin, accommodating a new pain, throbbing in wounded that were designed to not draw blood. I saw its left shin, blackened, dark purple. It had been cracked with something, softened. The body trying to cope, trying to fight the internal bleeding, the infections, as life tried to flow back into that dead and snapped limb. The bone was clearly broken, flattened inside the leg. It was designed that the onlooker, perhaps those to the right of the body, or those that soon be on the left could not assess the damage. Maybe only in the first moments of being tied down, or the last of being dragged out. Maybe these bodies arrived unconscious. The only other outward damage on the body to the far left was that the fingernails were missing.

I spotted a blemish on the floor of this barren room, and saw it was teeth. The body on the middle left had spat them, or they had been dropped from an implement. The bodies jaw was misaligned too, only just, but visibly so, unset. It had been broken with a blow from something heavy, I would guess. Where as the last body was one whole wound, a red, throbbing mass, these first two were pinpointed, even healed in places. Wound on the second body seemed surrounded by white scarring, fat and puffy. I discerned they had healed and been reopened. I imagined them all now stood, without these sheets and how they must have appeared to themselves. Beyond the pride they must have once had, perhaps just grateful to no longer feel the leather straps. But for now it was discernible they all took what breath and relief they could, and it did seem they were looking at us, up towards us. I listened for any noise, any groan or vibration. Anything signalling a call. Then I realised beneath the grate we resided in there have been a door. For how else would anyone access this gallery?

In looking down I began to notice a change in colour tone on the floor below. I could not see the door, if it was there, beneath where Greg and I crouched, but somehow the empty colour was emptier in an amorphous, borderless shape that seemed to trace from the floor up to the beds and then thinning out in flicks and slashes on the floor. Only be seeing the large patch of changed colour could my sight then discern the decorations on the floor and walls. It was so as though these parts of the room were just inflected with a single grain of luminous, perhaps toxic material.

A sudden movement, perhaps only a foot, or even a toe, from one of the beds, I could not see which, alerted me to a change. How long had we been watching them? Merely seconds perhaps, or far longer. Greg was still, he had not looked at me once to discern my reaction. His face seemed impassive. In this tiny gesture what I sensed was an overwhelming animal fear. This was made clear by the smell which began to emanate out of the room and hit me full force. At first, as I stared into the taut and ever tightening bodies below, I though it my own senses increasing in sensitivity, because, perhaps, danger and self-protection were in the air. Soon I realised the smell was more tangible than that, but not offensive. It was not I who had made up ground to the animals but those in the beds, who had evacuated their bladders and bowels. At least it seemed that way. No moisture dripped, no further colour was visible. All that was noticeable is that the third bodies hands, blackened from burns, without fingernails and it would seem with deep cuts up into the hand, between each finger, seemed to reach for its groin.

I heard the steps a long time after them, or so it seemed. The grating noise of the key in the lock below us, where there was a door, it turned out, seemed impossibly loud. The lips of the bodies started to move, in different stages of cracked and bleeding disrepair, so that blood began to spill, slightly and fully, bright, and painting their lips like lipstick. Into the room stepped a small, hunched figure wearing a dark blue pinafore and carrying a bucket and a white plastic case. It was wearing a white wig, or had curled white hair, tight to its head, of even length. It could not have been more than five feet tall. Its pinafore rested over a dress of a slightly lighter hue. It was long enough that I could not see its feet. There was a noticeable sagging of the bodies, though small, it was noticeable they were relieved.

The figure seemed obscene at first, perhaps because it seemed able to move at will while all else could not. Yet it did not move much, and maybe it could not. Its head seemed to blend into its upper body, if its upper body could be discerned from its lower. It tapered from the hair down to the floor, and it seemed to be looking for something. Then it placed down the case and pulled from within it a spray bottle. It squirted some sort of liquid on a tiny part of the floor and then crouching over, with a disturbing swiftness, used wiped over the spray. It then, never once changing the face it faced, as though it were fixed on rails to look upon the far wall, in the same direction as us, began to spray the feet and legs of the body in the first bed. What seemed like cleaning fluid was jetted onto the feet of the body, and then it was wiped off. The wiping moved up the leg, and onto the blackened shin and the body made an open mouth.

The cleaner worked its way across all four of the occupants. At times the spray bottle would be refilled, and then shoot out with what seemed in its tiny action, the only real motion in the room, to be punishing jet force. Sometimes the scabs came clean off under the wiping, leaving behind cuts or pink patches of skin. Other times they bled. Sometimes it would have to rewipe pus, and would do, until it ceased weeping. At times, as if accidentally, she would push and pull the bodies, each terrible minor shift causing immeasurable PAIN. Each time, their mouths opened silently. The implement, which I assumed, but could not see, as a rag, would catch fingers, toes, lumps, welts and raised cuts. And then the bodies in one sudden heave, were lifted, and their backs scrubbed, their arses wiped. Once that liquid mess had been drained and dried, then the body would be allowed to lie flat and with imperceptible quickness a new sheet was thrown out over them while the old pulled in. As though what was underneath could not be exposed to open air. Or someone watching on.

When the four bodies were cleaned, their lungs visibly heaving under their sheets, sweat mingling with cuts already running, the cleaner walked backwards to the case, and removed a clipboard and sheet. A pen clicked, and the sound of the nib on the paper, imprinting into the board was clearly audible. The bodies were becoming stiller, I could see though that in wiping the face of the third body, the cleaner had offset its nose, must have been previously righted after breaking and was now veering to the left. Somehow I was not surprised to see the body not seem to notice the change. On the first body the lungs were not settling, not returning to their shallow breaths as quickly as the others. Some wetness around the eyes, bruised as they were but open, not too swollen, and ceasing its writing the cleaner, as an afterthought walked back over to the body, having removed something from the case and laid a cloth over the eyes and mouth of the body. The cloth was white, not dirty, the brightest thing in the room. It was laid gently, covering the whole face like a caul or a mask. I then suddenly wondered what had the face looked like? What was the face beneath the cloth? What age, and gender? And yet I could not take my eyes from this covered face. A human face. With its other hand, the cleaner began to gently pour a clear liquid from an unmarked receptacle upon the cloth. The body strained, but not so much. There was no sound of gurgling, just a faint straining at the bonds.

Then I felt Greg was gone. He had left my side, but only moments ago, as I was transfixed. I could see his shape crawling ahead of me and so I followed. It felt as though we emerged back into the garden in mere moments, though it was not, and the purple sun, clocking down in the sky suddenly seemed quite traumatic, powered by some terrible suffering and not a machine or a virtual inanimation. I was suffering aches in my legs from the squatting, and I swung my arms around me in response to that. Greg had retaken his seat in the nook and sat impassively, I assume waiting for me to join him. What felt impossible was my doing so, fully illuminated, able to swing my arms, to feel my legs repair themselves, to feel not hunger or thirst, or pain in anyway. But I did so, and sat.

Just a cleaning today, he said.
I saw.
I'd not have you see the other days.
Not yet? I asked.
There will not be another other day, he replied.

I felt quite sick at the intensity of the flowers smell. This minor resting place, where no bodies were buried, suddenly seemed to me like a botanical garden, so full of obscene colour and scent. It seemed so artificial, the fusion of plants from utterly different origins. The great spidery dome of the banana tree made me feel horror, and the smell of jasmine was an insult.

They're real you know, he said.
I know, I said.
The plants, he said.

I followed the inflection in his voice on the word plants into looking at his face, and realised how rarely I did so. His long, grim bearing, once so recalcitrant, even feeble, to my eyes now seemed cold and aristocratic and intellectual. I saw before me a brutish face, neither better nor worse than the others. He was staring out past the garden, to flecks of dust or matter being thrown up into the sunset. Or so it appeared, they could have been the flotsam of the trees floating down.

You've noticed the dust before, he said.
From the incinerator?
What does it incinerate? He replied.
Objects of the museum, I said, as I had been told. Papers, dirty maps, used merchandise.

He raised his eyebrows and I felt the purpose of his gesture, looking for the first time with care on the floating ash. Not far from our boarding rooms, this little antechamber, I had first taken for a generator, then an incinerator, was something else, perhaps. It was harder, thicker than paper or cigarette ash. Bandages, excretions, offal, the refuse of the Museum, taken for the tree sheddings, on windless days, when thick dust smoke floated through the courtyard, irritating throats. The stale odour of timber rotting hit my nostrils, the buzzing of the electric wires from which hung speckled light fittings filled my ears. No flies though, in the garden. No spiders to eat them. No insects at all.

It is forbidden to be uncovered.

I know that, I replied.

That is why, even in those galleries, the sheets have to be changed so quickly.

I remained silent. He made as if to stand up, and leave, and return to his post, the last of the day.

Are they special? I asked. Are they the ones who demolished the Museum?

No, he replied. They are too young.

With that Greg stood, his long legs carrying him away from me, back into the corridors. I followed, but did not see him turn.

# JOANNA WALSH

# I WISH SOMEONE LOVED ME THAT ISN'T CAPITALISM

*"True, under capitalism every worker is manipulated and exploited and his/her relation to capital is totally mystified... But exploited as you might be, you are not that work." Silvia Federici, Wages Against Housework*

*"Capital is not a thing, but a social relation between persons." Karl Marx, Capital Vol. 1*

i.

*I'd love to write more of this story but my fingers hurt.*

It was that coming across the square to kiss you.
coming across the square to kiss you.

*Back in England, this is the first time I've thought of suicide for a long time.*
*Thought is the wrong word; I'm visited by the feeling,*
*Living in this house, everything still in boxes, it occurs to me as another thing that could be opened.*
*As soon as it is closed I disbelieve in it.*

(I didn't see myself, coming across the square to kiss you.)

*I have been, frighteningly, either content or unhappy. By turns. All week. Sometimes several times a day. I am content while doing house stuff. But I am sleeping too much, eating too much, drinking too much. I am bored. It is being here. I can't continue here. The register changes bit by bit. Drink makes boredom worse or, no, drink is more violent, utterly discontent. I can't make a life here. There is no life for me here. This is no place from which I can start again.*

What I saw was you getting closer, and I saw you while you didn't see me and I liked to see you not seeing me but talking to someone in the square while sitting there, so perfect I almost didn't want to reach you.

*The new place has become a matter of*
*Moving things very slowly room to room.*
*I even slept once in the afternoon.*
*Not tired but always sleepy.*

It was a long way across the square but eventually I reached you.
And, having been granted access to your body not only in bed,
but a hand on a shoulder, casually, in public, I kissed you like you
were something that was mine.
(As I approached, I took a photograph.)

ii.

*In the meantime, I've been having problems*
*With men*
*And their definitions.*

I was walking again across the square to kiss you...
(Don't look too loud, I can't hear you!)
When you looked up you said:
*Baby.*

*Online, one of them talks to me only about sex,*
*Another never talks about sex at all.*

*Baby,* is what only musicians call me
There have been two of them.
Neither is that other man but, as so often with men – with me –
there are always two.
Is that because I am worried one won't be there where the other
one ends?

*One man online called me a slut for fun.*
*He said I liked dirty words -*
*I'd never thought of slut as dirty*
*Only cruel.*

You said *you play bass like a girl* and I said, *I am.*

*(When I try to type 'men', sometimes I type 'me'.)*

iii.

*To stand on the brink of a person is exciting. It is also dangerous.*
*It feels increasingly dangerous. I have tripped over too many.*

I am buying many things. It turns out
my ex owed me a lot of money
from our primitive accumulation.

*To stand on the brink of someone is boring. Another person.*
*When I have sex and friendship, what need for more?*
*Love clatters between my hands to the floor--What is it? Nobody*
*knows--something loose in its workings, anyway.*
*But I must not wear you like a gold watch.*

I am strangely rich, the kind of richness that will not be replaced
Better enjoy it now.
I have bought a strange new bra with uncomfortable wires.

*My conversations with the men: no longer sexy*
*I am sleeping too much.*
*Catching a man is like catching a fish, a matter of luck,*
*But also of being there, rod in hand, waiting.*

If I can hang on here through the winter
Until my next friend's party.
It was only a week since the last, but –

*My interest in pornography as a currency via which I have exchanges*
*with these men. They like to know it though they always want to talk*
*about something else. They push me into categories: 'Ooh you're a rebel'*
*'are you 35? - No? - What age then?' 'I can see you're clever enough to*
*go to a top university! - Bristol?'*

Things like: I forget to walk the dog.

*But I am ready as ever to relax into the warm bath of certain phrases:*
*'Gorgeous!'*
*'In love!' (I am more wary of this one now)*
*They are all 2-syllabled and dragged out.*
*They are perhaps a kind of drag.*

Things like: I get fat or thin now very quickly.
(I always have a feeling I can shrink myself
Into the size of clothes that happen to be on sale.
I hurt myself trying to fit everywhere.)

*One man online said 'little' about me; called me 'my little' + art, 'my*
*little' + intellect. It put on a warning light but also - don't I want to be*
*belittled by someone not overimpressed? 'My little,' is what he said, like*
*my little pony. He put a claim on me; he tried to make himself bigger,*
*though In Real Life even a little pony is bigger than any human being.*

Being confused as to what I was, before we slept together I
had much of my hair stripped off, though you could probably
establish my class position by the variety of small snacks I ate.
But I was beautiful with you. I mean I found myself beautiful.
It was sudden. I was happy to walk around naked (despite its
being winter it was 20 at midday). It was strange, this being seen
domestically, going about my business from all angles, unmade
up. It had not happened to me for a long time. And I was thinner
than I thought. I didn't eat, (but then - I didn't work!). I looked
younger (I can't have! But I did! Overnight!). Or at least whatever
I'd gazed at critically in the mirror was no longer there (had it
been my critical expression gazing back?). Or the mirror was in
a dark room perhaps. How can I sustain existence in someone
else's eyes *dans tous mes etats?* (Or in mine?)

*I am impatient for someone who wants me in the flesh.*
*Just occasionally, any of them has sent me a black x in a white box, and*
*it has made me wet.*

iv.

*There are a variety of men I could call up and say, how are you today? This depends on distance,*

Baby!

*Back in England a man I know joins clubs I won't join. He joins book clubs, dinner clubs. He wants to be better, he wants to know me better: this makes him teflon. He goes to the gym. He has a personal trainer. He stays at hotels I find expensive, which he tells me are cheap. He works in media. He knows 'celebrities'. I don't like any of this, but what else do I have right now?*

Baby is a shutdown word, the hi-hat to a punchline,
'Baby.'
Say it!

*Back in England: Sale - nab your free mug! Oh, 'nab'! Like another man I was talking to who said 'mate' he said, and he was talking as if to another man in a fantasy in which he was sharing me sexually with this other man and he swallowed the end of the word like he was not himself but this other man, the man he'd imagined, or so I thought because he was no longer talking like himself at all. It was this I found erotic. Shortly after that he told me he'd been to an expensive private school well he didn't tell me in so many words but in so many more: he told me his old classmate was in the paper today but I didn't bite oh no mate no! tho I did look up who his friend was after and therefore found out at which school they had both had been taught, which is just exactly what he'd been trying to tell me all along.*

But, here. Now. Squares in the shadows. Revolution at point zero. No, the squares were the shadows. Inside them, light. And I say
that *love is an argument*
Because I need always to be against.

*What I like in men is the language of seduction, which you have stopped*

*using. Does this mean disappointment, or familiarity? I know one who*
*never stops.*

To reperform this paradigm
I must withdraw. But
Once they have had me
(that old saw)
It holds no water.

*Then there are the comfortable comforting men I talk to but don't want*
*to meet. Are they too easy?*
*(I will peep, again nevertheless, to see if any of them has spoken to me.)*

With: to turn to the other person and say, always:
*What shall we do today?*
(Having been granted access to someone's body. Not only in bed,
but a hand on a shoulder, casually.)
To have to do what we say we will, after we ask that question.
(To have, on the other hand, no variety in bodies.)
Or to have to say no.
Or not to say, but to wonder why it has not been done.
Or:
To take the phrase as the caress of a hand.
Our own primitive accumulation.
(Both our countries in disarray.)

v.

*Over that winter, that guy died who said*
*There are ways of seeing.*

What happened the day we met? I can't remember. This blank
in my memory disturbs me. Did we do it in the bed (surely
only once, memorably, the next day, on the couch)? What did
we do after? It was early, but I was so tired. Did we sleep (I
can't remember that we had any wine)? Did I read, write, send
messages (I could check the times, but it feels a cheat)? Will I
remember that first night accurately, sensually, later? I don't think

so: once a sense memory's gone, it's gone...

*That winter more people I know started to talk about their lovers. Not boyfriends/girlfriends. Husbands and wives are never mentioned any more. 'Lover' is an active, present-tense verb. Something going on, even as they type it, even if they're not doing it right then.*
*Or:*
*These are the people I know now.*

Grasp hold of the facts: he's in a taxi
The clamour of the future – beating in his head as it is in yours –
in which you are both famous
As you are both a little already.

*Their photos are bad things; they are made of light. I don't look up anyone's Instagrams; pictures invite a story.*
*And Instagram invites the very best. They have good lives there. Even when I know they do not.*

I don't know if what I have is an olfactory memory. I'd thought it was coming from my jacket but now it seems to be coming from nowhere. I'm being haunted by the ghost of a scent: to be precise, *Comme des Garçons Black.*

*Online one man is typing: 'You are a sensual woman.' I have no idea what to type back. I should reply, 'I like to feel things'. Then I should also reply, 'But I like to find words for these feelings'.*

This was also the winter my father refused any more to see my dog.

*Another man types something about women writers as witches.*
*As tho that were a good thing.*
*As tho their works appeared by magic.*

In the meantime, I am writing a lecture on true fiction.
I want to sleep all the time. There is nothing to go out for.
I am eating too much. There is nothing else to do.

*Where is this story taking place?*
*There are several answers.*

But sometimes we held each other as though we wanted to be held, just that, but the same, both. I can't think that was something I imagined.

vi.

*I am actually now frequently talking to three or four men at any one time*
*which makes things more, not less lonely.*

I am listening to an opera. I find the male voices hysterical. I don't like their vocabulary.
I don't like anyone's vocabulary.
These boring intrigues we cook up
So as to have narratives.
Before I thought I knew how to parse boredom.
Now I only feel good when at the mercy.

*Strangely I'm finding I don't like romance*
*Filtered through capitalism. One of the men suggests he'll buy a dress*
*For me that he can wank over when I'm not in it. I say nothing but I*
*think:*
*'I buy my own clothes!'*

Away from England I had not been able to distinguish day from day. They were all the wrong length anyway. And we never did anything, only drank and ate and wrote music and fucked. By the end of my stay you'd stopped talking about my English accent.

*I take too much care of men. When I have them.*
*I mean, treat them too carefully, withdraw, respect too much.*
*I am too careful of men, when I have them.*
*By which I mean both of these things.*

In the end, you said,

I'd like to fuck you but also I'm distracted.
Than you said,
I'm no good at goodbyes.

*Anything that can be replaced is a thing.*
*Any thing that can be considered to have failed can be replaced.*
*Anyone who can be replaced can be considered to have failed.*
*Anyone who fails is a thing.*

So here I am, back already: and I would like one material thing
to make me happy.
To locate love in one pair of eyes, one skin, one scent.
To trust to that, is more difficult here.
I am already beginning to archive our connection.

*(You have to look at who benefits. That is always the question.*
*You also have to look at who labours.)*

I am not content with these available men. No, I must find
someone who makes things.

*When invited to want things, I am quite capable of it.*

vii.

*How much it costs to have so very little, nothing bad enough to be hidden*
*away.*

I was in an expensive store writing a story called, *I wish someone*
*loved me that isn't capitalism,* when you texted me,
…*Baby.*
You hadn't texted me for quite a while; it was less than a week
but it felt like some time.

I'd sprayed myself with your scent unwisely. On the test strip
it smelt medicinal, nothing like on skin. Thinking its chemical
composition had altered I sprayed it all over me. Through half
an hour it changed to smell of you, and so did I. It's a tenacious

perfume: you always smelled more of it than of your body. Unsurprisingly it also smells of whisky.

It was the sale and some very awkward things were 50% off. They were large yellow cake stands and sweaters with fake holes and jeans that were too small for almost anyone. I walked around the store and somehow the idea had hit me for this story or not the story just the title which struck me as amusing and terrible at the same time, so amusing it made me almost laugh and so terrible it made me almost cry but at the same time I was writing it and that was pure good.

That was right at the moment I was staring at some oversized ceramic jugs shaped like animals with holes in the tops of their heads, where no hole is in life, to put liquid in, and holes in their mouths where in life there usually is some kind of hole, to pour it out, and tails curled round like handles. I'd got out my phone to make a note when I saw your text. I was also starting to cry.

But I knew I wouldn't cry a whole lot or noisily because all the time I was crying, I was writing.

# JAY
# BERNARD

# IF THERE'S ONE THING YOU LEARN AS YOU GROW OLDER

If there is one thing you learn as you grow older, it's that adults are physically different to children, but ultimately they are still fourteen, fifteen, twenty-one - we are still the people we were at our most formative moments. The changes we make to ourselves are real and true, but the children we were remain almost exactly as they were, waiting in a cupboard, coming out at night when we're in bed with our lovers and are inexplicably overwhelmed. I'm watching a film, and really when I think about it, the film is just some adults pretending to be someone else. I watch some porn, and the adults in it are dressed up and smooshing cake into their bodies. House shares are brought down because someone is reminded of their parents in the expectation that they clean the bath out after themselves. People hate other people because they can't shake the bigotries they learned as a child. We all spend hours each day, scrolling upwards, hating it and loving it, because, at bottom, we are children and the internet is sugar. We don't grow up, we grow flesh around the baby we were, the toddler we were, the child we were. We return to the ends after years in another country and it's like coming back to ourselves. We miss the ordinary things. The corner shop. The library. The park. To be a child is to be a super-computer. It is to inhale experiences, language, love. It is to operate with your body and mind intact. But most of us can't keep it. Either someone shakes it out of us with their violence, or we learn that we are a different colour, or that our attractions are perverse. Maybe a friend commits suicide for reasons you can't comprehend. It's only when you're older and you're sitting in the playground instagramming your old spot that you realise how much these moments mean. Just how much you lose, is lost daily, is wasted.

# NOW I'M NEARLY THIRTY I'M ASKED FOR ID ALL THE TIME

How do I make sense of my historical moment? The other day I finished tidying up my room and I found a poster from a project I did about Alan Turing. It reads "What does it mean to be situated in history, to exist in a particular time and place?" When I was under age, 15, 16, 17 I found it much easier to buy alcohol. Now that I'm nearly thirty, I am asked for ID all the time. Literally, every shop keeper is astonished to discover (when I hand over my driving licence) that I was born in 1988. I was made in the eighties, friends! But I look like I was born around 2000, apparently. Some people could believe that my ass was pushed out of my mother's vagina seventeen years ago and that I am therefore not eligible to buy this sweet, sweet IPA I am currently dependent on for my sense of self. A lot of trans guys experience the same thing. But I am not of this age. The older I get the more I wear my historical moment on my sleeve. People like us, we are perpetually teenage, perpetually ten years younger than we are. Except that when I'm around people born in 1995, 1996, 1997, I am ultra aware that this language, this identity didn't exist for me in quite the same way; I am aware that I learned about this stuff when I was nineteen, twenty, that my political awakening around gender happened when I was twenty-one, in love with a Canadian in Vancouver, at what is now understood as a transphobic music festival that closed down a few years ago. I went, and it was one of the most transformative experiences I have ever had. Have you heard of it? It was pitch black at night. People were generous. Everyone assumed you meant no harm. Elders loved me. They gave me a cup and a spoon and a fork. An older lesbian invited me to her place in the woods, and you know I still have dreams about it – I still dream about swimming in an open lake with someone twenty years older, trying not to drown in the dark blue current, drying off in the shower and having a beer later, and having to reconcile myself with her. Having to reconcile myself with the fact that she was always standing in a particular moment in history. Always. Aren't we all fighting for freedom? And aren't we all stuck in our particular moment, our pin-prick in history, our burning moment when everything mattered and everything was clear? I fear my generation doesn't have that. We have people laughing in our faces. We have trolls. We have people questioning whether we are adults. We have age checks and verification and blocks and measures and pre-emptive strikes and stalkers and gropers and disappointed parents and debt and violent porn and resentment and a strange sense that history has passed us by and hormones and talk of living forever and chest surgery and bum fluff and no pension and no savings and no mirror and no children.

# TIMOTHY
# THORNTON

# FROM: BIRDS, MAGIC, AND COUNTING

## 1. Protection against magpies, briefly

Magpies have always been extremely dangerous, but it was established as long ago as the middle ages that it is possible to protect oneself against them.

The technique still used today is to count aloud, up to and including the number of magpies present, attaching a word to each, making sure:

1. that every odd number and every even number are paired opposites;

2. that all even numbers rhyme.

e.g. *joy*[2] with *boy*[4], in the most well known version; *mirth*[2] and *birth*[4] in another. There is evidence that the first pairing in any spell must be synonyms for *sorrow* and *joy*.

Unfortunately 4 is as far as most of the well-known spells continues; *silver*[5] in the common version will keep you safe, if there are 5 magpies – but if there are 6, and the word used is *gold*, not only the *silver/gold* pair collapses but the entire spell. It's been suggested that enough witnesses to a magpie gathering will be reciting the rhyme that the protection is (as it were) split around the group, neutralising a larger group of magpies in groups of (usually) 4.

Recent researchers have conjectured potential continuations of the rhyme, sometimes as far up as numbers in the 20s, although none have been successfully shown to work. But it is an old problem.

William Blake was plagued by magpies his entire adult life, and the frequent occurrence of rhymes of 'joy' – particularly with 'boy' – in Songs of Innocence and Songs of Experience is thought to be directly an artefact of this. 'The Sick Rose' rhymes 'joy' with 'destroy' – it's not known whether verbs are effective, but nobody has discovered a reason why they shouldn't be – and we can also find 'joy' with 'annoy'. In 'Holy Thursday' there is even 'joy' with 'poverty'.

It is an attempt at a rhyme easy to forgive if you consider he was probably in fear of his life, facing upwards of ten magpies at the time.

You're probably wondering whether a different starting point might be fruitful: well, in the 14th century, nuns at the convent near Ely were working on lists of words rhyming with 'glee', and got considerably further, although above 34 they struggled to find convincing pairings of opposites. It's also known that monks in France were working on the problem even earlier; the spell isn't confined to English.

In fact, magpies have an equivalent spell to protect themselves from a given number of humans, which works according to the same pattern. It is equally effective but far easier to put into practice, since 'joy' in their language rhymes – as does everything – with everything else. This is one of the reasons they are so dangerous.

Please be wary, this autumn/winter, and consider trying synonyms for 'joy' if you see more than 4 magpies.

## 2. Protection for swallows, briefly

That *two swallows do not make a summer* is well known; it is less well known that this is an axiom, not an idiom. In fact, *any integer number of swallows larger than 2 makes precisely one summer*. It is more difficult to prove that *one swallow does not make a summer* but it is widely believed to be the case.

In the general case, there is some malign sky-ghost hovering by the outcrop there, which in a single inhalation exactly halves any even population of swallows, the sound of tearing and a shower of small bones from above, nothing else visible then a chaos of scatter and alarm among the survivors.

So in a summer made of a massive even number of swallows this sky-ghost may for reasons unknown destroy a huge number of swallows; that this loss is devastating is compounded by considering that the resulting number of swallows whether even or odd *in all cases except that of a single pair* still makes a summer. A massive odd number of swallows may seem to be safe, but take care to remember that swallows may die individually by other means; it is to be hoped that the sky-ghost is absent or distracted when one of a large odd number of swallows dies, leaving a large even number.

Now suppose the apparition again, and again, of the sky-ghast, feasting on a summer comprised of a number of swallows which is a power of two, until finally the number of swallows making the summer is 32, then 16, then 8, and then 4, and then at last 2. This, of course, is defined to be no longer summer.

Could the summer be salvaged, researchers asked, if the sky-ghast just halved this population? As mentioned earlier, *one swallow does not make a summer* is often heard, but this case is more properly said to be undefined. Experiments were done by starting with the assumption that *either remaining half of two swallows* might be said to be a summer.

It was found in any case that this was too late, because on the way to the specific instance of 1 swallow which is half of two swallows, it was obviously necessary to halve 2 swallows, itself no longer summer. And sky-ghasts themselves can only survive in the summer.

It devoured its final brace and as immediately as autumn fell it faded. Yes, at least there are some survivors among the swallows, and it is to be hoped that those survivors are very much in love with each other, but it is no longer summer.

Experts in summer are studying numbers of swallows which are one less than a power of two; experts in sky-ghasts are studying autumn. For now, if you must make a summer, make it with an odd number of swallows.

## RAGGED SIGILS

The other day I woke up and had in my mind the phrase "to stamp a ragged sigil on the sky", which seems to have something to do with what I'm about to write down. I wonder what the moon is doing.

Something nice happened this evening, related to something unsettling the other night. The good thing neutralised the bad thing. I'm going to write it down because it's keeping me awake. I'll probably write it as if automatically but in a voice which is a bit different from my voice because I still feel strange.

One morning last week I woke to find some scribbled notes. I'd forgotten about them. But then I remembered them. And now I remember at the time thinking that I felt a bit mad. And that I had been feeling mad quite a lot lately. The way I'd been feeling mad quite a lot lately was to do with feeling like I wasn't anywhere, except what I was thinking. And what I was thinking had mostly been the same, and it was not somewhere it's possible to be, really. It won't be easy to describe. I will say five things about it.

The first thing is that the scene is a pane. Where I am is a pane. And the pane is enormous, so that it may as well be a plane, since it seems to go as far as thought can go. Except that since it seems to be made of glass it is also a pane. There are marks on it, or through it, which I'll come back to. And the pane is moving back and forth in space enormously fast. So that if you were on the pane and had ears you would hear air rushing past them. But there is no air and no you and no pane. You are the pane because it is everything there is. So that actually it seems still because after all what is it moving through.

The second thing is I want to mention the shimmering patterns you may get if you have a migraine. I think some people call them auras. These are difficult to describe and surely are different for everyone. I have no idea. When I haven't had proper sleep I get them. They start as a small dot somewhere in my vision of bright white light, which slowly gets bigger. As it gets bigger it is not a dot but is a circle or a loop, or a part of one, like a filament of bright light which is also a shimmer. And the shimmer seems to be made of triangles. Although the triangles are fixed to the dot or filament somehow, because part of it, they are in a way moving back and forth or swivelling enormously fast. After about twenty minutes I can't see a thing. And I can't see a thing for maybe ten more minutes and then it passes. And I often feel suddenly oddly exhilarated and energised.

The third thing is: supposing these tiny swivelling triangles could be zoomed in on with an electron microscope and were somehow made of glass, well, that is the pane I was seeing. It is everything I can think, being fixed as a tiny speck on a swivelling triangle in the shimmering aura of a migraine. As a sort of window, or visible region, in the style of a microscope image on the pane of an imaginary triangle. And since the speck is tiny the swivelling is dizzyingly enormous. Even though all seems still, because all there is is the pane.

The fourth thing is the pane is riddled with cracks. They are all through it. The pane looks as if it should shatter or fall apart but it does not. Some cracks are long and cross it for unbroken distances. Some branch off, and branch off again, and branch off again. Really alarmingly often where three cracks meet there seems to be a chisel-mark on the surface of the pane. As if this has been done deliberately.

The fifth thing is that this is not made-up. I knew everything about where I was right away each time I was there. These things about the pane and the triangles are not similes. It is simply where I was. I did not have to try to figure out what these things were, or where. It just takes silly time to write it down. That is the place my head was in. Maybe I was right to say I felt a bit mad at the time. I'm bored of describing this place.

★

I spent lots of today looking out of the same window. It was the window you look out of if you're in a flat that two of my friends live in. We had all been having a hangover together. Outside was faintest traffic roar, occasional voices. Every now and again and more prominently there would be some exchange of bulletins between the gulls, but not enough to be annoying. The sky was blue and still and almost cloudless. At least, there were clouds in the sky in the same way there were children's voices in the air. Which is to say they were not quite comprehensible or distinct.

And I mention the the sky because it was a crucial part of the noise. By which I mean the silence. That zero-plane which feels on such afternoons as this like it's behind and through everything, blue and roaring. Because anything that's blue and forever must be roaring, even if it's silent and still. Everything held taut in invisible thread. Or a spider web perturbed only by the slightest breeze. And all sound emerging from a sky-blue roar of flat silence like the back of a dolphin and then returning to it. And the gulls going ka, ka, ka, ka, ka, ka, kaaaaa.

We recovered slowly in all this, with coffee, and fish-finger sandwiches. Because of the time of year, the colours of what was outside the window changed almost every time we looked back at it. Always to something differently beautiful. The sun wasn't visible in the window as it set. The buildings we could see looked very glad to be reflecting the sunset.

It got very quickly a great deal darker and the moon very suddenly appeared. Really very suddenly. You will know if you've ever seen the moment where the sun sets that these things really are moving very fast. Anyway the moon was behind things. A distant crenellation cut rectangles out of its lower half and there was a prominent ridge of dark cloud slicing the top off. So that the moon briefly looked like a glowing chamber suddenly there on top of this building. An alien installation maybe. None of this has much to do with anything.

Soon the several trees to the front of the scene outside of the window were by now absolute blackness. Indistinguishable from each other. And indistinguishable as to whether in front or behind. All their branches had become was an interlacing of crack-patterns, as if flat on a plane. The plane also containing lozenges whose colour was the yellow glow of street lighting. I realised as I moved slightly further away that with the tops of the trees obscured by a large piece of scaffolding all I could see was a framed area, with black crack-patterns branching right through it. And obviously I'm going to say I shuddered to be reminded of feeling a bit mad and being fixed as a tiny speck on a swivelling triangle in the shimmering aura of a migraine able to see only crack-patterns, extending in all directions.

I didn't say anything. Immediately, as if I had, one of my friends said something. He said he had been trying to describe such a pattern but had not been able to think of the right word. And that he had therefore invented one. Perhaps together they had invented one. In fact that's certainly correct, they had invented it together. I won't tell you what it is. Mostly because I can't remember it. But also because it felt like being let in on a very tender secret.

Perhaps it felt that way because of the sheer relief. I wonder why I am writing this. Relief sounds silly. Much about what I am like at the moment, and what I write, is silly. And I feel like I want to apologise to anyone reading, to claim I did not need to write this, which would not be true. By the same token I'll say relief.

I felt right away that if ever again I feel like I am a bit mad and am fixed as a tiny speck on a swivelling triangle in the shimmering aura of a migraine able to see only crack-patterns extending in all directions then my brain will rescue me by doing a freeze-frame, and fading, from the image of crack patterns in that hectic void, to the image of some dark tree branches growing through each other, in a pitch-black web, seen from the window of a very safe room. And to the memory of being in the company of two people I love very much, who had found it necessary to come up with a word for this pattern. And who told me what it was, without my asking.

# JESS ARNDT

## SERAPE

He moves. It's like someone's poking him. He moves again. The pillow is damp. He rotates, tender. Wet everywhere. One eye cakes open, pupil seizes *en guard* against the light – he's alone.

He could have sworn a man...

En guard! He shouts again and falls back like a plank, could be deceased.

Both eyes open now.

Morning.

He blinks awhile. Same mean mattress (his), same mushrooming stain above him. The plaster is leaking. One drop of water rolls around his ear's fleshy inner tubing. He listens to it *drip drop drop*. This water has a stalactite's insistence. Imagine the caverns of my brain, he concocts, where a driblet is thickening, pear-shaped, lugubrious until finally it's so heavy it must...!

A stalagmite catches it...!!

But a worse moment comes on its heels. An oven. Light cruises in freely. His heart bucks. *Did we colonize the sun??* If he was really *thinking* he would wonder about the leak and the sun – at odds. But he's not. Can't think with this spotlight on him. Plus there's something he doesn't want to know yet.

Oh but here it comes anyway like a 999 steam train.

MY CLAIM.

Better if it came slower. In the Netherlands there's record of a train pulled by a dog.

Nope it's here. It flattens him. He'd like to never get up but the blankets crawl over him patchily and his whole body is roasting. He tips and teeters. One leg down. Feels like he's standing straight on his ankle no foot.

Doesn't she (landlady) have the pitiful class to lend him a rug?

The littlest things cause his brain to ejaculate with torment. He's going to go demand a footpad. Plush. At the very least! He searches the room for his clothes. But nothing is easy. Did his dorm-mates mug those too?

He stares at the raw wallboards. The fir smell is choking him but he's trying to picture a green forest. The foliage so nude and spongy. Slowly it occurs to him that there's weight on his body. He's wearing them - miner's jeans. Canvas drop sleeve shirt. Boots even. All of them freshly bought but now they feel pasted on.

Well forget the basin. He's too shaky to shave. He shoves his hands again and again in his back pockets, trying to turn them inside out. Nothing but sand.

He coaxes himself down the stairs like he's 80. At the landing he lunges sideways, attaching himself to the rail where the molding, hip-height, meets the wall. The boardinghouse is narrow, cigarlike, same color too.

I'm suffering, he says.

He wants a table by himself but it's just Zoilites in rows and rows and rows. Finally he sees safety, a stool by the kitchen door that the landlady sometimes occupies, mean and rugless. He gets there. His knees bend. He catches the stool top with his butt bones. Now his teeth are chattering.

No big surprise. He drank his gums off! Breakfast smells like herring. Oily drifts boff the air.

Elbows on his thighs, plate in his lap, he glares at each Zoilite (if he can even separate them) with exactly the same measure of suspicion. He's looking for the smoking gun, some beardo waving the stolen claim at his neighbor, some sphinxlike countenance or a bottle of 'bou passing around before its usual appearance at noon.

But is it before noon? Who can tell?

The shadows bend in subterranean patterns and he swears in the corner someone's hunched on a lamp, making it glow. Well fine, he slept all day. Wouldn't you if you were poisoned, kidnapped, robbed?

There's a constant buzz going around the dining hall but he can't see a single mouth move. It's like beetles munching wood, he thinks. He glares again at the mass. For once it's easy not to talk.

Yes Pinkie? he says anyway. Testing his voice out.

But he doesn't answer. Instead Pinkie looks down at the fish. It's quivering in what he can only guess is pomade. He sucks up a bite and the greasy bone hairs dive at his tongue.

I'm done! He tosses his fork. He remembers with a lot of conviction – there's a serape he wants to buy out there on the street.

He's not sure but the sun has either set or it's stuck behind a blob of fog. It's all fog blobs here. If he was going to write something that's what he would write. But who uses language like this, *for describing*. He walks down Dupont St. taking big resolute steps. Suddenly his bones? Jelly.

Well that's just a shiver?

Yeah fine, ok, it's night, he says.

Who knows why but he's driven to the serape vendor, the one he saw yesterday. Of course there are umpteen hundred of them. So why care which? This particular vendor wasn't even so good…just a chubby guy from down north.

He doesn't investigate the feeling. But he passes two or three peddlers laying their striped ponchos out before he settles into an ok pace. He knows there's nothing special here. That the serape vendor picks his gear up from the warehouse just like the other guys and the warehouses are filled from the clipper ships, the ports, the farting burros, the ferocious drunk it took to get over the mountains and before that toddlers crawling over the yarns sucking cajeta *god life's boring!* etc etc.

All this time he doesn't think about the claim once.

He doesn't think about Valapai either. It's been snipped from him. Or maybe, like an umbilical cord – someone left it hanging until it dries and falls off.

Don't even go there, this guy was never a baby or even a kid. What was he even doing in Valapai? Who knows. Completely not the point. The happiest he's been was at the party with the saltpeter miners. That's it.

Out here he almost can't believe the noise. Frisco's blabbing her mouth! It's dark as maté and nippy and lanterns and coal fires brew up everywhere. He's counting the streets now, he's sure he's about to turn down the right one.

A strange thing is forming in his mind. He wouldn't call it a thought.

I don't know, he says.

He pauses at a beer hall.

Well maybe just one?

He actually pushes his tongue out and dampens his lips. C'mon they're dry. The pinchers that have been grinding down on his head all day find their meat just above his cold strawberry ears. He's heard about the north Pacific – all gluey seas and its giant man-sized crabs.

He swallows. Now he's sure a smooth sac has enveloped his insides and holds the inner grid of his body separate from his skin. The skin is the same as always. But what's in the sac has been monkeyed with, punched around. Little sparks and dislocations flare up any place the sac and skin touch. Am I just stargazing? he wonders. But it doesn't feel good.

He's going uphill now, he hates climbing, the beer hall is right there – he could always give up. But way off ahead: he does see one lamp blowing back and forth in its own closet wind.

Omphalos! he says.

It's one of those words he likes on sound alone, no idea what it means.

The lamplight seems to lather up the street. He speeds ahead, even sweats a little. Sure enough there's the serape vendor. A stupid looking guy but he's certain now – he's the one! It's a strange place for a vendor though. Ie over in this corner of things, up a steepening hill. When he looks back down the city seems far off, abstracted. Peculiar thing about walking.

It's probably got to do with this shitty hangover! he says out loud.

He's convinced the serape vendor can't hear anything because the wind is blowing. His cart is tilting sideways on the muddy ground and the vendor has placed a large rock in front of each downhill wheel. Pinkie shakes his head. Such a dumb place for a cart.

He's not doubting himself but he'd like to grab the serape and get off of this vacant incline. He notices trees now in a clump.

The street just peters out. Can you believe it? They haven't even built this part of the city yet. But now he's here. No talking – just a lamp and a cart. He's intent. He paws through the ponchos – can barely see them. Color at night? In Frisco they do everything crazy, he thinks. Each one he pulls out looks just like the others. He's tossing them to the ground, the bank of damp wool grows.

The vendor doesn't budge, just watches. He isn't chubby after all. He's just wearing many serapes on top of each other. In fact his face is lean. But now there's nothing left, Pinkie's hands hit the bottom. Don't ask him to describe the serape he's looking for either, he'd have known it if he'd seen it. He pauses. The lost claim and now this. He's going to insist that the vendor undress. After all, he'll have chosen the best one to wear himself.

They stand there, he and the lean-faced serape vendor, the bare cart between them.

I'm suffering, Pinkie says loudly.

I'm suffering man, he says again.

He keeps saying it and saying it and saying it.

## DEEP DESERT

The stadium lights switch on. It's 4.30, the time I always go outside. Past the doorjamb. Under the carport, there's the desert. Sky is mutable lilac, glowing back from Big Bear. I take a picture, knowing it won't represent. Then another and another until my phone dies. Clouds are lapping, wrinkled, layers. Like a product description I read earlier today for a soft pack dildo: "over 89 authentic folds."

I'm in a bind. Can't or won't write. Each day has the most gelatinous pace. I get up with a modicum of integrity. Swish around. By 2pm I realize I'm in trouble. Will be dark soon. Now the chimes are going, getting the smallest push from what up north they are calling *rainpocalypse*. "Won't fix the drought" everyone is in a hurry to say. Last night I did something different - packed the fire with a big mesquite log then this morning just stirred it to life.

But even as I'm writing a heavier wind starts pouring down from the southern hills. It's five weeks since I've left Brooklyn. Enough of the layers of dry expanse. Of course I want a storm.

My friends are on an island called Fuerteventura: strong winds. We skyped for an hour plus. I don't know why I note this except to account for time. They were so tan and salty and sleepy from wind surfing. "Who's with you?" I said. They typed so as not to be overheard: "seniors. *Over 60-no, over 75's*." Other things we discussed? Prince's entire discography including early "jazzy" stuff. Ferguson, as in - can a racist society teach non-racism to cops? Mass protest and its effects. I've been reading Wikipedia. "Have you eaten goat yet?" I said.

I wonder about my homebody-ness. Feel like I should be out hiking, that kind of thing. The feeling comes with a visual of the word - "mastery" or maybe "domination." A boot claiming a hill. That's what you're supposed to do when you encounter a landscape: own it. At Rocky's pizza (blue vinyl chairs, smells like potpourri) the guy in front of me opens his billfold to pay. I haven't socialized today so it's easy to stare. He's muscly. Shaved. The cards show he's from the military base. He also owns it. Power.

Last night my New York cohort talked about writing as pursuing wildness. Now I'm immediately embarrassed about those last few lines. An idea being - how to write with politics that don't collapse into rhetorical moves or language. "*I know*," I say. "I know."

Over on the nearby couch my copy of "With My Dog-Eyes" by Hilda Hist. I like her tradition as a writer of "the obscene." The obscene, says the translator's preface, in Hist's formulation, is: "differentiated from the erotic and the pornographic by its philosophical and spiritual elements, and also through it's act of social provocation." It was time, said Hist, to "wake people up."

I flick on the outside lights. It's dark now. There's a truck going up the dirt track. It's been my most enduring fear out here that a truck will roll into my driveway, idle, turn off. Enduring because I've encountered the others. Hundreds of tiny black widow spiders, the obliterating 3 am quiet, a chain of fights with new loved other, writer's block.

But 29 Palm-ers like using these trails for their 4-wheelers. I hear them out there revving - chewing up the desert. It's the addition of the dark, the wind, the rumbling of test bombs that makes me pull inside, re-check the doors, etc.

I crouch down by the books. All the good titles. Crowley, Bataille, Genet. These were Hist's favorites. My friend whose house this is has put them in order by color. It feels like a kind of pulse. The colors emblematic, as in, this author's visceral news is represented *like this*. I am not wearing the packer I already own but if I was, this kind of position would have made it fall out. *I think in a past life I lived as a goat herder*, I tell my girlfriend. *Look, I can crouch like this for hours!*

*Uh huh*, she might have said.

But she's in LA, 3 hours west. To get there you drop down through the mountains and the air becomes damp. Right before the gap there's a Mexican restaurant, La Casita. It's festive. There are Christmas lights and booths. I went a few nights ago and someone kept calling on the phone for someone else named "Carl." "No we don't know him," the waitresses said to the caller. "No, *he's not here!*"

I also love Crowley (black), Bataille (red), Genet (black: "Our

Lady of the Flowers," white: "Saint Genet" (really Sartre)). Open on my desktop, an unread essay by Philip K. Dick: "How to Build a Universe That Doesn't Fall Apart Two Days Later." It's over 8,000 words. I can't possibly! But why not, I don't have a job. I DO get to paragraph two and his one sentence answer to the question: *what is reality?*

"Reality is that which, when you stop believing in it, doesn't go away."

Last night another friend calls and leaves long messages on my answering machine. He's been drinking. He wants me to write about my Brooklyn apartment (where he's staying) and his dog. But that's impossible. I know too much about my apartment, his dog. I can only write about myself because it's obvious that no one has any real self-knowledge.

I sleep again, barely. My girlfriend and I are arguing about something so small that it won't go away. Then I lie in bed for hours, paralyzed, thinking – where can I possibly go next? No job, writing's flat. I seem to have escaped my life. From out here alone in this hermit-stance, anything feels like crawling back. At 3am a mob of coyotes start going crazy out in the yard. They all sound like babies, ravenous babies, yipping and crying.

Today the house's desert-pack foundation is rattling, the single-paned windows shaking like teeth. Now the bomb sounds are bigger: it's Middle earth being rent apart. You know where everything splits open from the grinding of horrible stone wheels and everyone's whispering *"the ring, the ring"* and what are they called – wargs, orcs – pour out? I've been trying to play that word (wargs) in scrabble for days but it's always all vowels, no luck.

About the truck that idles out there in the drive. I'm calling it here, I know I am. I decide to watch a Herzog documentary: "Into the Abyss." It features two men. One of them is on death row. When they were teenagers they killed three innocent people so they could go joy riding in the red Camaro they then stole.

This was the 90's but *is it* innocent to live in a walled-in community, to own a Camaro? When I'm trying to sleep the eyes of the now deceased Michael Perry keep coming back to me. "We wish you the best of luck Michael Perry," Herzog says, in that waterproof way of his, knowing the kid is going to die. Michael Perry is smiling but his skin is so pale and his irises are round and black.

Prince liked red sports cars too, Corvettes, who doesn't. But last night my house was full of the apprehenders' pickup truck vibes. Shotgun blasts, *wrap the body up in silk sheets! Dump her in the lake.* My fault, I'd told them to come in.

2 pm again.

Now it's 3. The internet's down from the weather. I'm annoyed, relieved. Since I showed up Nov. 1 each system has wobbled – the firewood too green, the propane tank empty, the well on the fritz and thumping constantly, the irrigation dumping swimming pools of water – oh yeah and the plumbing and septic kaput: the pipes are full of maxi pads! Explained the plumber knowingly.

"Reality is that which, when you stop believing in it, doesn't go away."

I'd finally sequestered the idea that creatures were living in the couch when I watched a scorpionlike body scrabble across the floor and up into the recesses of the coffee table, to safety. It was tail-less. They don't have poison, just claws. A "wind scorpion" they're called.

Prince, the wind, the Camaro not the Corvette, the appearance of the bug.

One time in a defunct story I wrote:

"Sometimes there's another logic we're forced to follow when we can't see any deducible way how the writing is jumping from A to C because the jump is contained only by the breathing body writing this."

But all these things do seem so connected, so blatantly.

Days spurt forward. I leave the desert for a brief reprieve. North. But not before my friends (whose house I've been renting) suddenly decide to get married and with my black plastic internet-born Universal Life card that I keep in my wallet I'm getting ready to minister vows on the shortest day of the calendar year in the space that I now have to part with, that I have scrubbed and arranged so tidily, that begins to fill with party people - strangers - for whom I pour methodically-made champagne and whiskey drinks, then usher outside to the desert floor to sit in and around the ceremony that I have somehow mostly written.

There's the crowd. There's the desert. "To have no clue, no idea," I say. "To make things without contingency plans, to mimic any number of cacti weirdly pointing, to brain out in every direction, to huddle and collapse..."

The same me who hours later puts my hand through the cocktail serving jar and bleeds copiously, then, encouraged, spits booze into one of the many scattered outdoor fires wanting it to roar, who, excited, changes it out for mezcal that I pull from my car's trunk after earlier promising myself not to, who still later sprawls in the sandy yard on my back ruining my "minister" shirt, saying "why? why?" at the body standing in front of me - genuinely, furiously, for a brief but encompassing moment unloved - ?

"...to practice disobediently," I say. "To practice with each other, to do it in and with, because of, in exaltation to: the umbra, the dusk, the dimness, the dark..."

There's a cake cutting, a knife dance, we're zipping off small fireworks inside, there's ceremony.

But I'm a train that can't be stopped, this not-so-foreign version of me who having gone too far insists on beer can after beer can, inhales midnight leftover carrot soup, begs physical absolution from the same adversary/consummate lover on a pullout couch with what feels like extra limbs or no limbs, band-aids for knuckles, who wakes up shakily, ashamed, face grilled to pancake-thin mattress at wintry dawn.

Is there another way to say goodbye?

Last year I wrote a story from a similar condition. About a fermented Mexican mash called *pulque*. A six-year relationship was simultaneously nodding out and exploding into abridged but terrible bouts of fighting on frigorific Brooklyn streets. I was erasing myself nightly in the most composed way I knew how.

"When we drink, we take something in to leave something behind," I wrote. "I think."

How the passage isn't free. How the same Thoth card I had

been examining then appears now, a year later: *The Moon*. I'm in Washington State, as far north and west as you can get and still somehow be in it, on an island that's so reclusive that unless you know someone you'll never get here. An island that is right now as wet as the Mojave is dusty. Black-green trees guarding the beach as we pull cooler after cooler of supplies from the boat, lichen-coated everything making the bark and stumps and plastic tarps that cover the machinery ghostly white, froth on all sides of every wave. One day a nor'easter the next a nor'wester, then wind from the south, it keeps scouring for something, moving around.

The card is described by the Thoth bible, Mirror of the Soul as: "you're passing through sinister sentries whose heads are those of wolves" but then is, in the same breath, small surprise, a vagina... "changeable, moist, shadowy, seductive, possessing an eerie attraction. Everything appears mysterious, doubtful and bewitching." My girlfriend and I go out walking. Big mermaid-y hunks of bull kelp, gulls screaming at us, a clump of shiny-eyed seals who stare and stare. A rock emerges on the tide-savaged sand, somehow it's both oval and triangle-shaped. The granite composition makes black pubelike speckles but running through its center the material is fleshy pink - an obscene thick slit. We're on a sandy finger protruding seaward, in front of us a mess of waves, then Canada, that's all.

Christmas morning two lambs push out. I carry one of them out from beneath a mammoth storm-broken cedar. She's all legs, *she weighs nothing!* I hold her by the belly and realize the wetness is from her umbilical cord - frayed and hot in my palm. I'm used to appendages like these. Floppy, half-alive Frankensteins. "I take it back," my girlfriend says. "I DO wish you had a dick." She says it on a dark slippery path, there's literally a burial plot just ahead. It's romantic to me, she's talking about coming inside her, I know what she means.

The next day at breakfast my dad beckons me outside with his squat forefinger, his double-wide palm. I get up from the family table. I know where we're going, I don't want to. We walk up the hill, past the machine shed and barn on our right, the cosseted orange and black Kubota tractors sitting in the temporary sheep pasture on our left. He's whistling, he doesn't mind our task. The mud is thick, I can't commit, I won't get all the way dressed, a small resistance – my socks already soaked *take that* – I'm in someone's mismatched crocs.

We stand at the pen. He's been up here already today, divided them – the older sheep in one area and then the eight yearling lambs. We have to pick two to be sold and butchered to our friend S. Some of them are twins. I've mostly conquered my lifelong fear of pair-splitting but now my mind is racing to invent empathetic math. The pen's tight, the animals are shaking. "Which is the smallest?" My dad asks. I point. "Which now?" I point again. I'm holding the gate, he's wrestling them out.

You're not *god*, I say to myself over and over. But it feels like I am.

My dad's swearing, giving me familiar orders "you HAVE TO SLAM IT closed!" they're running at him. I'm suddenly worried about his body. Didn't he wreck his shoulder? And what about his trigger finger? The slipped disc in his lower back? His work-mangled hands?

"Type A, Type A," my brother and I sometimes chant for relief, confer about how his heart must be cranking. "But when I'm resting my pulse is at 42!" he offers proudly if you ask.

It's done, I walk away. He's happy, he loves completion. I don't want to show him my face. The two I've picked are alone, calming down. I can tell they think they dodged something, they're safe. It feels real, the gruesomeness of the choice but simultaneously I'm wondering: is this just a bizarre-o gender performance? Is it really possible that you – at 36 – don't want your dad to know you're upset, see you doing *something like* crying?

*But I was just eating a handful of bacon!*

(*Is THAT a gender performance too?*)

The full moon is in cancer, or almost. A cranky highly sensitive moon – you might take it all very personally. Something about entrenched family dynamics. Walking back down the road, firs drooling their black frondescence over me, I'm apart from nature, have done bad things, more muck in my crocs, it's pouring. When I re-enter the kitchen my mom, a vegetarian, tries to make me feel better, says: "They're all going to get killed anyway so it wasn't really a choice!"

A passageway is compression, a channel, something you slide through. Yesterday the wind was screaming and the sea was all milked up. Now from the nailed-in desk in my 10-by-15 cabin, the water is silvery, flat as my lost Mojave view, as if waves would be impossible to muster. What happened in the in-between? I played cards, got drunk: tequila, whiskey then a large blue glass of stout, raining again. The windows of my tiny 4x4 truck wouldn't close. I didn't care, they were steamy, I kept jamming the electrical-taped handle, the boughy trees pushed in, junk and relics leered from the woods - from the places they'd been stuffed years before - I was or wanted to be lost in the night.

"*I'm still trying to remember whose idea the Irish car bombs were,*" my friend, last name Connor, texts.

The same friend who over cards, in the kitchen, with the cook stove sweating, couldn't stop talking about the book *Santa Was a Shaman.* How in Nordic countries a million years ago priests in dyed red furs squeezed through the chimney holes (that were also the door holes) and pissed psychedelic mushrooms into the mouths of their villagers.

A memory jerk: backyard garden party in Brooklyn, somehow drinking a past girlfriend's urine from a plastic cup, our second date. "That's nothing," she said as I swallowed. "My *EX-girlfriend* let me cut her with razor blades on our *FIRST* date."

Did I survive puberty? Like really survive it? How about the second still-evolving gender one? It's not hyperbolic, answer's: no. Not the same me.

My friend emails, the one whose desert house I was living in. It was "wedding as performance," a Green Card wedding, we smashed a piñata to papery bits with a stick and peanuts came out, the ceremony was so long the cold sun *on cue* set, I said "with the power vested in me by aliens, Laurie Weeks, whoever…" At some point it became real no matter what we did. In the email she tells me her truck skidded on black ice off Old Woman Springs. The truck is totaled. It was 20 degrees in the deep desert. No one would stop and then when they would stop, 911 wouldn't come.

How many places can we be at once? I take my own truck and start driving across the island on the wrong side of the road. The truck's Japanese, it's built that way. My cousin's leaving, we're rushing to catch the only boat off. The road winds, it's not pavement - just a rug of dirt and mashed fir needles, seems redundant to say it: more mud. It's 2 pm but up here, twisted up in the trees it's *already* dark. Around another bend, I'm gunning the engine, my feet slipping on the clutch - *gotta get there* - a nameless panic filling my mouth, anxiety inherited from next door, from my father's shockingly lymphatic pulse - *gotta! Get! There!* But there's another vehicle chugging up ahead blocking me, a 4-wheeler pulling a little Rasta painted cart behind it, oh no, I'd know this cart anywhere, on the rear end there's the boxer dog drawn over the top of the flag - he's smoking a thigh-sized joint.

I'd honk if I could but the horn's broken. *Pull over CMON*, of course, it's S. and the lambs! I'm stuck behind them staring at their little bouncing white heads. What am I supposed to learn now? I'm driving like some sweaty sink-less Lady Macbeth. Can't wash the blood off. But S.? he's the happiest guy ever, plus handsome - *muscles like ropes*, he's from Burkina Faso, he speaks French, if I had to die I'd want him to kill me, I'd fall headless smiling, he's got such a convincingly melodic voice.

Later that night we dance at a New Year's party in the island's only community building, the still-functioning post office - an 1890's log cabin with an oil drum stove. Party's theme? "Address Unknown." It's half the island, there're forty of us packed in here, all ages but really *all ages*, 3 to 80-something in wool everything and wet boots, materializing at every door like apparitions from the 70's in our best party attire, fug of weed, fire, sweat, island garlic. My brother's djing, some kind of murky brown punch gathers its pistons and injects our brains again and again, now it's S.'s favorite song: *c'est la dance du chiens* the dance of the dogs "YAAAAAAAAA *WOAH*!" I shout so he shouts, we're both on repeat going nuts spraying our fingers up in the air, wind outside *or is it OUR HEADS* moaning but I'm dancing with S., I love it, I figured it out: *just don't mention the lambs!* Somewhere down the dirt road below us, the sturdy dock and CAN YOU BELIEVE

THIS LIFE???? the sluggily phosphorescent sea. I wake up what must be a few days later to my dad out slaughtering the rest - Jan. 1, 2015 - year of the sheep.

I go into the pantry, there's a large metal bowl of organs soaking on the chest freezer.

A neighbor comes by. "I saw your lambs up there bleeding out from a tree!"

In the kitchen, my dad's stooping over a pan, frying hearts. "Want some?" He's misty and relaxed, his butchering knife dangling from his belt in its orange rubber sheath. I get a plate and allow him to shovel me a few crispy rounds. I chew slowly - trying to taste them all the way, greasy and rubbery but also tender and gamey and sweet - but still swallow them so fast they burn my throat.

When we finally boat off the island they're trussed in net sacks, headless, hide-less, so firm and compact. I touch their cold chests as I load them on. Thanking them or apologizing or just muttering, I'm not sure. No surprise "The Silence of the Lambs" was my gay root movie - I'd watch it again and again so I could pine over Jodi Foster and her pain.

Back on the mainland we drive to a diner for breakfast before I fly south. Bacon again. The lambs lie out in the bed of the truck.

Desert house number two. 121 sunfair road. This one is farther out. It abuts US military land completely. A skinny calf-high barbed wire fence marking the line. It's a small adobe house built by a fag "Omar" and his brother. Also a pig pen, a goat shed, a chicken house, and old 70's bus with "ODD JOB" lettered across the front. The bus is filled with tools and porn vhs tapes. My friends come over, the same ones I married. We drink beer and start prowling the bus with flashlights. It's cold. One friend, the Peruvian, is wearing a Russian fur hat and trench. "Take everything," I say. Leather harnesses, wrist cuffs, wall phone cords (the curly plug-in kind), rusty hammerhead hammers, saws, kneepads, porn mags in German, animal milk collection jars, t-shirts that say: "gay punx," honey. Omar is gone. "He's not dead!" My friend shouts across some piled up salvage. "*He's just in*

*Berlin!*" But it doesn't matter the *true* truth, we can't stop talking about him like he is.

Meanwhile a friend croaks from cancer and I didn't call him. Outside at night alone with tequila and so much sky, I am aware of him passing not away but by. Dale "didn't give a boho fuck," was "an enthusiast"—the elegies are good. It's true, he didn't give a fuck! Was an enthusiast—it seems like possibly the hardest thing to be.

Crowley's still hanging around in my mind. Occultist, necromancer, occasional dick sucker, mountaineer, founder of the religion Thelema. I'm using the cards, trying to find my way. He named one of his daughters Nuit Ma Ahathoor Hecate Sappho Jezebel Lilith Crowley. But was he actually *bad*? I need to know. A few weeks ago in Highland Park, LA we were across from a house where he used to party, do séances, etc. Big porch, heavy shutters. We all agreed—it felt "dark." Now I'm taking a survey, I keep asking: "was he? *was he?*" "Crowley *was* a social climber!" my Peruvian friend says—the opposite of an enthusiast aka the opposite of vulnerable. The stars feel very far away.

Outside there's a white trailer propped up on tall black tires. It's the last building I investigate when doing my rounds, checking the property. It feels like it's been dragged here, left in its orientation for no particular reason. "Heather's" studio. I can't see it, then I can. I approach when the sun's setting. Time? now closer to, but not quite 5 o'clock. It looks like there's been a fire or a dark wave plus bacchanalian rager or a transformational ceremony involving long candles, wigs, witchy things. Outside the door: rusty bed springs but with a pillow carefully laid over the top, empty unidentifiable bottles, god's eyes in sun-split cardboard boxes, books shredded by someone, something, a ruthless wind.

It's getting bad over here. I'm comfortable and full of doubt. I know my way around the towns, the minimarts. Could chat functionally to multiple groups or individuals, even know some of their names, their "ways." The woman, for instance, who bursts into the health food store to let everyone know a dog's loose on the highway. She's the same one who, at the local café, laughs too loudly when spreading the news about the 29 Palms school kids run over (killed) by an out of control driver. I move a stool down.

Her mouth's perpetually open. "I won't bite," she says.

The trailer feels different from everything else. Twilight's short, gets snuffed out. The doorknob has a rope wound round around it to keep the metal door from banging. I unwind it, look in. It doesn't feel good. Something's unsettled. There are ripped up garbage bags all over the floor. I look farther in—a desk under a small horizontal window. A half-full bottle of Rossi sweet vermouth on it, capped. The desk's wooden chair is bound by a heavy leather strap plus buckle, like a wide seatbelt. My chair in the house also has a rope looped onto it—it's frayed nylon, yellow. Makes me think of that writing cliché everyone knows: when desperate tie yourself to it. But out here, after days of digging through fetish objects, flags with strange symbols, broken things etc., the belts take on other dimensions.

What's the word for when you're not doing what you're supposed to be doing but you just keep doing it and doing it? I can't settle in out here although it's easy to inhabit. Daily tasks mound up but are pointless. Things like: should I go to the dump (the guys are "nice," you get to drive up a trash mountain), or not?

On the weekend some Swedish friends show up. We hike and cook, they take lots of photos, it's pouring snow in Stockholm. They keep asking me how I'm doing. The question seems casual but they ask it a few times. "Do you ever get Lappsjuka?" "Huh?" They describe it: "a mind disease from spending too much time in Lappland." The word, "Lappland" is out of use now—offensive, they tell me (but lappsjuka persists). It's not Lapps but the Sami or Saami people who live up in the very far north. I do a google search—find reindeer sleds, real ones with leather and sinew and bone, that kind of land, my chest aches, *what about* the red-furred priests?

*"Ok fine, Mojave*juka," I confirm.

It's raining when they leave and fog coats the creosote bushes. Up close, their shock white branches crossed with tiny black horizontal lines look like something from "Beetlejuice." My fire takes a frustratingly long time to build. I keep blowing and choking. A stifled feeling, I can't see the horizon—mysterious how the desert closes in.

Now I've been alone for a string of days, a week. "Heather's really sex-oriented," my desert friends say. We're at their house drinking red wine and listening to a tape deck. I'm hyper from my silence, asking this and that, telling about a hulking silicone dick lying just past the burnt foundation (and tipped over stucco outhouse?) that may or may not have belonged to an exploded meth lab. The dick's on the ground, sand-hued, camouflaged—just "there." More about Heather: "she won't acknowledge you unless you touch her." When I first walked around the trailer I felt conscious of including something in my perimeter, in my smell trail—aware that until I encircled it, the trailer was other, apart. Should I unwind it, dis-include it from my path?

I'm afraid of my tendency to tame, my desire to put in place, resolve.

Still reading Hist. The book is small: "Libitina said the priests would go nuts. One of them poked his fingers through the holes in the grating and pinched frenetically at the tips of her nipples. Jacinta would get wetter and wetter and weak in the knees. Later the sacristy...

...Praised be the quietude of mine in this instant."

It's late, time to go. I get in my car, there's a night vigil where Utah Trail meets highway 62 for the kids who died. A big cross with paper garlands on it. Candles in clumps all over the ground. Police guarding. I drive under the flat night sky. Turning onto Winters, now the road's sand, pale-dark. I'm remembering I forgot to leave any lights on ie, made no contract with the house. Larger meaning: the desert owns it. It's cold and empty but something more than that—is sealed off, could be hostile or at very least unknown. Ideas scrabble by like nocturnal things. What if I pull into the dirt driveway and a light IS on? What if someone's sitting at the (non-existent) kitchen table when I walk in the door? What if: "Omar's hooome!"?

A neighbor's guard dog runs the length of, lunging at, his cagelike fence. Not dead means no spiritual visitation. Plus, Omar was a friend of friends. *Omar is home* would mean celebratory drinking? And bitching about? At very least some healthy weed in front of the woodstove. But what about privacy—mine? His? Yesterday I saw a raven perched heavily on a post, then immediately a single coyote. He sensed me watching. Stood very still in the creosote bushes. Something felt awful. I thought: "some days it's terrible being seen."

# MIRA MATTAR

## NEVER THE BLADE

It was the middle of the year and the weather was everywhere. We were lucky with it and knew so with our skins and also because we kept saying *we are lucky with the weather*. And that was the conversation. Supposedly, we were of the age where the marking of time by making 'progress', that is, reaching the regulating milestones and naming the gorgeous desires mere follies of youth, seemed to correspond with gumption and maturity. The desire (both material and spiritual) and ability (both material and spiritual) to pull off this particular adulthood depended upon your attitude towards deviation: was it abhorrent and crusty or was it a logical and allergic devotion? For many, going along did not feel like acquiescing, but more like: getting everything you've always wanted. Arrival. It is nice when what you understand as truth, lies, at least for the time being, without friction alongside the world's big story. For others, it was a shoulder shrug at best and a betrayal at worst, resulting in a soft eyed focus on the lovely past, drawing from it the capacity for emotional intensities necessary to tone the present day to day. It was the mournful comfort, yearning and suburban, of those who have designated criticism adolescent and pleasure childish – forgetting these as the gravest insults. For the rest, those whose existence itself was contrary, acquiescence was not an option, material or spiritual. They were neither welcomed into that heavy fold, needing as it does the enemies necessary to define itself, nor desirous of it, knowing it was incompatible with their survival, in that: it wanted them dead. Skirting the peripheries in the half light then, these ones oscillated between certainty that the entire order of things was arranged for only a particular type of life, and doubt that their very senses were trustworthy detectors. Me, I could not tell the difference between agoraphobia and claustrophobia having nourished with pride for so long my best error: knowing what is impossible for me above knowing what is possible.

It is easier to comprehend bunting if you admit that World War Three has started. Here it binds the trees, sags comfortably from corner to corner, pins the structures to when things made sense. What was this place? Bizarre in its construction as though the base rectangle had been appended and extended in correlation with the growing trend for large weekend parties performing their pre-nuptial rituals. Curious, brick and confident in a way that belonged to a certain class in the 1980s. Convinced of its polished windows and white sills, of its high ceilings and generic contemporary furnishings, of its decking and grass, of its hot tub and its rules. Was it built for purpose, a party house? Or was a new shell slipped over the old framework of a stately family home? Full of husbands' borrowed cars the driveway was slick as we arrived unwed in the loyal, chugging Toyota Starlet, fresh with country mud. This village was home to one of the country's biggest racehorse training centres and a rehabilitation facility for injured jockeys. To the north was a Bronze Age burial ground with over 26 types of barrow: bowl barrows, bell barrows, saucer barrows, disc barrows. As usual, I was in it for the vocabulary, loving the words more than their referents, how things could not come alive without being spoken – my shallow and murderous habit. We unloaded ourselves, our luggage and the slew of empty crisp and biscuit packets we'd wedged responsibly into the car doors and my one ally turned her back and morphed into her public self. Four or five steps led up to the enormous door which was swung open by a competent and clean-spirited woman with good hair and a shirt with embroidered flowers – to playfully undercut the seriousness of its blue stripes, it's Saturday! Like the others – tight-jeaned, fair and milling slimly about inside – her left hand had been weighed down with a ring of formidable heft, sure to blind any rival. The way they talked about their husbands was inseparable from the way they talked about their ailments – my IBS, my PCOS, my hernia, my ruptured disc, my nervous breakdown, my husband. The atrium was vast, bypassing each floor until it reached the ceiling from which swung an enormous 19th century style chandelier of entirely unpredictable provenance. Was it valuable, antique, or a cheap and local replica? Stairs swung up and round in an easy spiral depositing guests onto the landings of the three floors from which branched the 10 or so bedrooms stuffed with some 30 beds. Grand, tacky and engineered for maximum fun. The tones throughout ranged from neutral to pastel, an occasional lilac, a milky green. Entertaining rooms plush and cosy branched off the atrium on the ground floor as did the kitchen which had a table large enough for 25 people (seated) and windows rising from above the counters up to the double height ceiling. Off it again was the well kept, uptight garden, behind which was a real field stocked with real horses who were really shaking their hair and neighing and munching grass in the unseasonable weather. I have never felt romantic about horses. My adolescent friendships with horse-loving girls were necessarily limited: those girls possessed a faith and power which I admired but could not touch – and it seemed a fundamental touch; and I possessed a capacity for looking not only to the bottom of things, but also inspecting them from every angle, which they needed occasionally but also feared, not seeing how doubt could also produce motion. I preferred the intricacies of spiders, the dubious communality of ants and bees, the tragic arc of pupae to butterfly. The rooms had been allocated and thankfully I was with people I knew. The whole genital vocabulary of riding bored me. Was the association between 'female' sexuality and horses, which seemed entirely classed too, really clitoral or only a fantasy of men? What was the appeal? Was it about the ambiguity of control – the creature's or the crop wielding mistress'? Was it about becoming one undulating muscle moving in a perfect communication? Was it about freedom? Whose? How free can a domesticated animal be? How free can a girl be? Was it only a fantasy of freedom, or did it contain fantasy's intellect – able to at least imagine being unshackled? Was it the safe thrill of ownership edged with the fear of loss? Or was it about the simple, sensual, terror of trust? And there were carousels too, and rocking horses, My Little Ponies and those mechanical horses outside shopping centres and corner shops in the towns we got born in, waiting outside kicking dirt or left in the car with the window cracked.

*It is not for us remember, it is not for us.* She with her ideal hair getting combed along the shoulders. *We are here for the happiness of another, our own unhappiness does not matter. That is tradition so please tell me if these polka dots are too daytime?* Once my dearest, lilac-eyed, she found me excessive then as she does now, yet it is this that keeps her towards me, a direct channelling to the marrow at three o' clock in the morning. To me depth never felt like descent. Into me friends open the fists around their insides: the secret breast, who should not have been seduced, the necessity of murder. I do not know how I became that portal. I just as much want what is up there in the street – old man transfixed by a flower erupting from a wall, coil of fox shit dappled with blossom petals. But here I had to be fun, that is: perform the almost impossible feat of simultaneously drinking alcohol for hours and hours *and* staying awake. Acknowledging every angle without adhering to any one is what makes me a better friend than romantic lead. Romance likes answers, but friendship – the only relation unregulated by law? – falls over itself with permissions, possibilities, questions. It can be the most intimate distance, flexible. But friendship too can solidify – through neglect, or through the subtle changes and betrayals that linger unacknowledged, unincorporated. Love in itself is not a structure. Like the paw of the cat in its adorable comedy I try to push things open but they remain closed. At some point people just want to get on with it. At some point what is liked best about someone becomes despised. At some point if you keep talking about it, people will stop talking to you. And now look, she's talking to herself? I liked to be thorough but did not know the names for anything. With no language beyond a nervous one my conscientiousness became obsessive. Always only an amateur, fanatic – but who knows what manias heave unbidden inside the good exteriors of others. *Can you please just stop pointing things out and relax, the weather is amazing and I have four days off in a row.* We'd nursed each other accurately every evening, and during the lunch hour lay entwined regardless of envy. Love was an almost total lack of disgust. Rashes have charmed me. Now I was somebody else's child. Why wouldn't she come towards me? Was it the time we used to have? Was it ambition? I wanted our clothes to touch but she shoved hers with a near matronly efficiency to one side of the wardrobe. Once again I had not realised the kind of shopping that was required – particular fabrics and qualities of fabrics, recognisable shapes, nothing second-hand, the dissection of the body into assets and liabilities and the subsequent play of revealing and concealing. I long ago picked food over figure. Who am I to feel so free? To be different to old friends and still hang around is to get called 'quirky' – the name they give their feeling that is the mixture of disgust, envy, fear and pity. To be different to your family and still hang around is to have the cheek cupped first with pride, then slapped with shame. *Please suspend yourself for the ceremony,* she says with my mother. *It is because you brought them up in 'the west' that they are both unmarried.* But mother, the cruelty of here is still preferable to the cruelty of there; father, I am as homeless as you but ultimately it is gratitude that overwhelms me, that overshadows the guilt of trying to go at my own pace, the luxury of abandoning god. It translates into 'when are you going to make us happy?' their perpetual question to unwed women below say 35? (I riff on crone and carrion to no one.) Genuflect and take your medicine. It was the women who wanted to sedate me most. They knew that we were always the fabric and never the blade and that pride alone could make this tolerable. I was trying to make the hate come out politely like I'd been taught: as nerves, treatable. I couldn't believe the fuchsia of the pill. It was unladylike to hate, arrogant – if arrogant for a woman meant critical. Though for the men it meant learned – they would dissect out loud the rituals, their tribal origins and relation to property, women and class; they were half listened to and revered vaguely, all the while getting poured into identical suits by their wives and mothers. I listened, but it was not possible to perform the sister analysis with my stuttering body – as though intellect did not spring first from the sensory world (if not from the body, so often muted, distant, a stranger's). Theirs was the vantage point of distance, lending the men a seductive safety I kept slipping to – but they could not tell that the knife was at their throats too, too far from themselves and blinded by it to see it held in their own hands. Caliginous, sloppy, my cries were inchoate. What will really be more disruptive – the maid of honour quitting, or the albeit true witterings of a man in a suit indistinguishable from any other, easily distractable by a buffet, a short skirt, a toddler? It is once again true that the more threatening what someone has to say is, the more formally they are ignored. *This is not about you.* The discomfort of some is often the quiet buttress of the comfort of others. There are as many ways to feel uncomfortable as there are options for wedding florals. I had been practising my disguise (personality) my whole life so my techniques were perfected and my likeability intact. I had the advantage of excellent camouflage: ethnic ambiguity and a man by my side. Was I dishonest, spoilt, or in hiding, sensibly? For some, happiness is individual, for others there is the anxiety of wanting 'everybody' to be happy. Because this is impossible, these people do not throw big parties, but make for conscientious guests. But we learn how to party as we learn anything. Now we know that party doesn't mean the exclusion of all day to day activities. Wash up if you like, tend to the plants, be still. Being together is hard. Almost every woman I know in Amman is on anti-depressants. They joke – they should put it in the water! But the joke's logic is flawed: they cannot drink the tap water. There is a photograph of me from that cousin's wedding that my mother treasures: under the floral pressure I appear slimmer than I am and with straighter hair (*you look much prettier like that*), wearing the alien costumery of large scale wedding industry and a smile made sloppy from the pill. A complicated heartbreak is playing out: she looks at the image and sees the daughter she wants, the equation of 'my daughter' and 'femininity' is finally balanced. Beauty in this image is the correlation of a human being with their assigned role. I cannot redirect her admiration towards me because really it is a feeling she is having with and about herself. I know my real smile from a desperate one. In the image there is only the beauty of efficient violence. What was my discomfort? Did I want to 'be myself'? A notion that is not universal or trans-historic. It necessitates first a conception of an individual self, then the possibility of knowing it, before finally trying to be it. Besides, here, it is required – the currency is authenticity, uniqueness, affective skilfulness, meaningful revelation and strategic self-actualisation. There, the imperative is politeness, respecting your elders, knowing your position in the social order and not deviating from it, or at least not too publicly, *though did you hear there are two women living together in…* In both cases, survival kills. Perhaps I just wanted to minimise the face's betrayal of the mind. I wanted to get myself out of the way, to see other people, and without only what has marked them, but conscious of the scars. A feat particularly difficult to achieve with men – either I see all vampire, or no vampire at all. I do not care who my mother sees in the photograph. We crack each other up in the supermarket even and that is a glimpse of the pervert's intimacy, which must first turn away before returning. Selves dissipate, and there they really are, or could be. Her eyelashes bloom thick and long into the wand. She pulls back, beautiful. *Can I borrow your mascara?* She hesitates before handing it over – knowing I'm part daring her to refuse, to show the narrow mind of her private hand. We both almost don't want the readying process to end, always the part with the best temperature. *Shall we go downstairs?* Clicks her clutch shut and tucks it under her arm. When did this happen? Real job, proper salary. Me: horny yogic scumbag googling pension advice for freelancers. Still, I want our arms entwined. She opens the door, *come on*, turning her lovely back.

It was a surfeit of plastics:

https://www.lastnightoffreedom.co.uk/hen-night-shop/novelties-&-accessories/willy-straws/
**Pack of Ten Willy Straws**
**Blow me!**
- £1.99 £3.99 save 50%
- Pack of 10
- 20cm long

*Extremely* detailed

If you're sipping your fluorescent pink, pure-alcohol cocktail through just any old straw on your hen do then **you're doing it wrong, buddy**. Everything and anything that can be turned in to a phallus should be turned in to a phallus on a hen party, and that definitely includes a long tubular thing that you put in your mouth and suck on.

https://www.lastnightoffreedom.co.uk/hen-night shop/products/drinking-buddies/
**Drinking Buddies**
**One stud of a bud**

£7.99
- Six pack
- Hunks in differently coloured trunks
- Effortlessly adds sex appeal to any drink

It's a fact of life, and there's no getting around it; **drinking alone is sad**. The weepy woman in the wine bar, nursing a Pinot Grigio – sad. The bloke sat in his bedroom, watching Friends box sets with a **crate of tinnies by his side** – sad. But not you. Oh no. Even when all the girls are away on romantic city breaks with their other halves you'll never have to be alone again.

https://www.lastnightoffreedom.co.uk/hen-night-shop/novelties-&-accessories/leroy-love-doll/

**Leroy Love Doll**
**He loves to get blown**
£9.99
- Black inflatable doll
- 26 inches high
- Black hair and a broad smile

When it comes to finding somebody to keep the bride company on her big night you can't find much better than Leroy. This travel sized love doll never stops smiling and he is bound to become the life and soul of the party.

What is this fun? How is it classed? It it bawdy or what is termed wrongly as ironic – the new loophole through which to safely enjoy the old conservatism? What is the intention? Titillation – to return them flushed and horny? Blushing, virgin again. Does this defamiliarisation estrange the 'male' body, to enhance perception? Dick as device? A refortification of the binary. Or is it a way to obfuscate our desire for each other, for a dickless relation? Is it to mock and make less threatening, to, literally, belittle? Is this advice for wives-to-be? (Because love's secret name is power.) Is it revenge? Is it the softer version of the men's parties – they get real organs and we get simulacrums? All our desire can be is the mediation for a stranger's orgasm. Is it to reinforce the reproductive? Is it to reinforce the human? Because one colour only is human, all others must be specified, falling outside the category of flesh. At best this is a festival of bad sex, at worst a murder scene: organs amputated, blown up, breasts cut off, hearts scattered, clinging, cannibal. Imagine if it was the guts, with which we also love, strung out into a straw to drink from. All this grotesquery but I am the nasty one for sneaking a smoke in the rose garden, bare feet, the worms! Hippy! The stars giddy out here in the country that I hate – never able to belong and not wanting to, never able to belong so not wanting to, never wanting to belong and not being able to, never wanting to belong so not being able to. What is it to be owned without belonging? What is it to belong without being owned?

Is the hen party the drab and logical destiny of the ornamental pink flamingo? Three hover inflated over the game of first kiss first fuck first fight. The story is ready and a line. Sweet, tentative, manageable. What has happened to the pink flamingo? First perched unironically in affordable tropical elegance on the working class lawns of 1950s Massachusetts, they moved from elegant, to tacky, to queer (via John Waters), to hip, to camp, to ironic, to postmodern, to the ubiquitously motifed animal they now are – adorning the homewares and decorative sectors as well as the clothing of children and adults from Primark to Prada. Some commodities are produced as kitsch, some achieve kitschiness, some have kitschiness thrust upon them. From the American housewife's lawn to the lawn the bride-to-be dreams of, with its accompanying house, car, husband, child, children – impossible to believe in. The women and I exhale into this pinkness sheer. Haha what do you where do you aren't you haven't you oh really that sounds nice lovely great terrible horrible awful dreadful appalling I'm so sorry congratulations. Hunched over the alcohols. Snacks in bowls. Cutting the room in teams. Did the ugly and cruel fights I'd had reveal the ugly cruelty of my relations, or were there truly situations in which the biggest fight was mere charming aggravation on the way to the vineyard left or right or who is in charge of the sun today or how many instead of any at all. Were these the fights of the saved? Where the limits were tacit knowns instead of unintentional excavations, accidentally discovering at any moment the shattered spine of another creature underfoot. I never knew the difference between antagonism and analysis. Therapists state sanctioned and private, free reiki from E, yoga with Adrienne on YouTube, kept telling me to 'drop down into my heart', that is, out of my mind. For me there was no difference because they were both made out of language or experienced as such. Better advice would be: drop out of language. It's a switch I need not a doctor. Now the game is two touching circles with smaller circles in their middles and even smaller circles in their middles two long ovals two slightly smaller ovals inside an x with lines around soft rounded w with an arrow pointed a long u with its top part sectioned off two stick people one with triangle one without a heart the game is the done thing the done thing is the game. It is a common story, the negotiation for freedom. I wanted to hear everyone's voice. But here I was leaning so far out, unwilling to affirm a thing, unable to squish back into the natural armchair, crouched on the floor silent under big science. Am I in danger? Am I dangerous? Was it a necessary danger? Why couldn't I have *fun?* And what is an enemy when your thighs are touching and you are wondering together what the cocktail's unplaceable ingredient is dill? And what is my body if it enjoys the hot tub, the dessert? I am the nasty one for taking part with the curiosity of a scientist. Spy, traitor. I see their lives as unreal somehow (a fantasy?), and they see mine as unreal too (immature). But theatre is only in the eye of the beholder. Feeling real is a luxury. The difference is only how well we will die.

## NOTES

The passages on horses and flamingoes are informed by John Berger's 1980 essay 'Why Look At Animals?' in which he addresses the history of the human-animal relation.

'Who am I to feel so free?' is the title of a song by MEN from their 2011 album *Talk About Body*.

'….as though intellect did not spring first from the sensory world' is an adaption of Helen Keller's phrase, 'for in touch is all love and intelligence' from *The World I Live In,* 1904.

'It is particularly hard to do this with men – either I see all vampire, or no vampire at all' borrows from Sara Sutterlin's *I Wanted to Be the Knife,* 2015.
'All I hear straight women say is
I love MY vampire
mine is Fine.'

'All our desire can be is the mediation for a stranger's orgasm' is a line from Maria Klonaris and Katerina Thomadaki's 'Manifesto for a Radical Femininity for an Other Cinema', 1977.

'...tropical elegance' is a phrase used by Don Featherstone, the designer of the pink plastic flamingo, to describe their reception on first appearance in 1957. This quote and related research comes mostly from a 2012 article in *The Smithsonian Magazine* entitled 'The Tacky History of the Pink Flamingo'.

'...impossible to believe in' refers to a line from Lisa Robertson's 1998 essay 'Pure Surface', 'Like one's own childhood, the suburb is both inescapable and inescapably difficult to believe in'.

# VICTORIA BROWN

## A GIRL CALLED JOHNNY

The TV pauses at the end of the ad-break. People running with carrier bags, loud hailer police shepherding them away from the scene. *That's The Cure holding down the coveted number 49 spot in your festive fifty.* The gas fire burns one arm. She folds another edge, allows the paper to find its own natural folds, runs her fingernail down each crease to sharpen it. Equilateral triangles of repeated Santas and holly. She snaps off more Sellotape[1] with her teeth and sticks one side down. The doll has real blue eyes, it can cry real tears[2]. You can still see the picture on the box through the tissuey paper.

At the other end she makes matching folds and searches for the Sellotape. Have to get the perfect sized piece. It splits, goes in the wrong direction, flips and wraps around her finger, sticks to itself. She tries to hold the paper folds down with one hand and unravel the tape from her finger with her teeth but it gets stuck to her lips. She lets go and the folds unfold. *Not a vogue-ish band of course, and maybe that's to their advantage, that's Orchestral Manoeuvres.* Ambulances are arriving at the scene. The edge of the tape has gone missing. She spins the roll in her hand. Her thumbnail is a stylus trying to detect the end. This time she gets a clean piece, sticks it to the edge of the fireplace for safe keeping, refolds the paper and tapes it down. There aren't any more presents to wrap after the crying-doll so she pushes them all under the pretend tree, baubles shake. Johnny pulls herself up from the floor.

1 Sellotape is a British brand of transparent, polypropylene-based, pressure-sensitive tape. Sellotape is generally used for joining, sealing, attaching and mending.
2 Special features included weighted eye-lids, which slowly close when she is laid horizontally, also known as 'rock-a-bye' or 'sleeping' eyes. Recommended retail price £7.99

She fills the kettle[3] and spoons instant coffee into a mug. Two mugs from last night are still on the drainer, coffee dregs in the bottom, lipstick around the top. She leans against the counter as the kettle gets louder. Johnny picks up the men's magazine that women love to read. Y marks the spot.

*Fiona was posing for these pictures and then she started using a vibrator on herself, says P. from West London.* Johnny rubs her left eye, smudging her eyeliner more. *I'd never seen her do that before!* She tries to get her fingers through her hair brushing out the

---

3 The advent of lightweight yet durable and heat-resistant polypropylene coincided with the re-emergence of the jug kettle, which has become the dominant type of electric kettle. Functionality rather than style has characterised the jug kettle.

hairspray[4] from last night. *Fiona is 40 and 36-28-36.* The electric kettle clicks off. She fills her mug and takes the coffee and the men's magazine that women love to read.

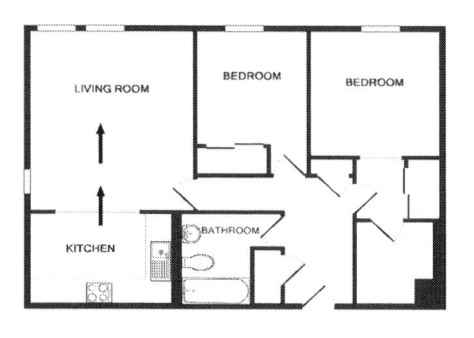

Sitting down on the carpet by the gas fire, Johnny puts the men's magazine that women love to read on the floor in front of her and sips the instant coffee. The pretend tree lights light-up the men's magazine that women love to read in multi-colour. The woman is kneeling up on a bamboo style settee. *Not a great favourite of mine I have to admit, but it's you the Great British public that makes these decisions.* The cushions on the bamboo style settee have a palm-tree foliage pattern. She's wearing a sheer black peasant-style blouse[5], black stilettos, stockings and suspenders. Her miniskirt is hitched up to the waist and she isn't wearing any underwear and there's a record player in the background and pictures of waterfalls and horses on the walls. There's a clock with a pendulum that chimes every hour. The men's magazine that women love to read says her name is Sandy of Berks. Sandy of Berks is smiling straight at the camera. Johnny drinks instant coffee and turns the pages. Sandy of Berks in her kitchen with her legs open and no peasant-style blouse on. Sandy of Berks in

4 Hairspray became popular and mass-produced after the beauty industry had noted that aerosol cans used in World War II for insecticides could be used as a dispenser for the product. Hairspray is a blend of polymers that provides structural support to hair
5 A woman's blouse, based on traditional European peasant dress, with puffed sleeves and square neckline.

her living room bending over the settee with no mini-skirt on. Sandy of Berks sitting naked on her staircase holding the receiver of her rotary dial telephone[6]. *If there are two words that sum up the Fiesta ethos, they've got to be 'sexy fun'.* Johnny leans back against her own settee, which isn't a bamboo style settee and glances at the TV. The Chief Inspector talks into a microphone. *Sandy of Berks took up the challenge to all those reader's wives out there, rolling around her home in the nudie before we could say Jackanapes[7].*

In the living rooms of 3,284 deck-access homes, each one with advanced underfloor heating, all trees are pretend trees[8]. *So far we've had two from Echo and the Bunnymen, and we've had two from The Birthday Party this is another from the Cocteaus, if it was up to me, if it had been my chart, this would have been in the top three.* Policemen comfort distressed women with no carrier bags. Johnny runs her finger through her hair again, it's all matted with hairspray. She really needs a brush.

6 A rotary dial typically features a circular construction. The shaft that actuates the mechanical switching mechanism is driven by the finger wheel, a disk that has ten finger holes aligned close to the circumference.
7 A cheeky or impertinent person, a tame monkey.
8 Most artificial Christmas trees are made from PVC plastic. PVC trees are fire-retardant but not fire-resistant.

Johnny flicks on the 100 watt bulb. The bedside drawer smell is a mixture of wood grain and *Charlie*[9]. She finds previously combed out hair wrapped around her main brush in amongst a small mound of face-powder, tweezers, *Tampax*[10] and hair-ties. Switching off the light illuminates someone's bedroom light opposite. The woman leans over a mirror, mouth-open in concentration, applying eyeliner. She kisses a bit of tissue and shakes up her hair. In a wrap-around towel, she flicks through her clothes like records in a box. Then she walks straight towards Johnny, looking out. She closes her curtains. Johnny can't see anymore.

9 Charlie is classified as a floral-aldehyde fragrance. It is composed of citrus, bergamot, hyacinth, green leaf, tarragon, peach, and aldehyde top notes, cyclamen, carnation, orris root, lily of the valley, jasmine and rose middle notes, and sandalwood, musk, vanilla, oakmoss, and cedar base notes.

10 The initial discovery of the telescoping cardboard "applicator tampon" was developed and patented in 1931, Gertrude Tendrich, then bought the patent and started to produce tampons, expanding from sewing tampons at home to distributing them under the brand name Tampax

# NISHA RAMAYYA

## FAINTING AWAY

A gold and ivory mace was positioned in one of her hands,
level with her cross-hatched waist.
> Your grandmother dreams of shopping for bridal jewellery.
>> I want to be ready for the last night.
An ascetic walked up to them in a smoky blue-lit cave. They
didn't ask how long he'd been waiting.
> Your grandmother dreams of a future in which going home
> is not growing lean.
>> My ghosts will come before flesh.
Her face was blurred but the position of her arms suggested
that she was smiling.
> Coming before 'vaster attitudes', you proceed from doubtful
> love.
>> I'm in without fading, mmm-hmmm.
The news ticker read: 'NOTES THROWN AT GIRLS
DANCING ON STAGE.'
> You imagine yourself to be eye-level with girls.
>> Wanting my (eyes closed as empathy).
An ascetic warned them of the 'impending destruction' of
ornately carved wooden columns.
> You call out your bad cause of a self.
>> Please stand up, please stand up, please stand up.
Five kings stood in a crescent, looking up. They prayed to a
goddess for protection.
> You don't want me 'so that the past could remain precarious'
>> When she will ask me to-ooh-ooh.
A bearded man in pink and gold prayed beside a tree. He, too,
looked like he was asking.
> Nothing heals your father like you do.
>> Hello mister, ah.
Opposite, the silhouette of a goddess. She promised to take care
of him as a daughter.
> The second change, which takes place in warm milk.
>> Uncertain as to which of the two.
The newspaper headline read: 'Congress men for chemical
castration.'

'What can I do my darling but try to speech' ghosts.

If I knew you were coming, I'd have tried to speech.

The big word 'honour' was pasted obliquely, issuing the smaller words 'police' and 'seething'.

Your heart from breaking our country back.

Hello mister, ah, how do you do?


Ornately carved wooded columns repeated themselves in a smoky blue-lit cave, issuing warnings.

The house that keeps your hidey-holes.

There, there, and there, ah!

A goddess held the heads of her enemies in each of her hands.

Your favourite action figures on the other side of the barricade.

Release me, release me.

Her skin became much darker; she took the form of their names.

You are hard upon anyone, 'So distant – to alarms – '

And though my love is.

He said: 'HO! A MERE FEMALE!', foreshadowing his defeat at the hands of a goddess.

To render downhearted, brown-hearted parenting.

And though my love is ooh-ooh-ooh.

The verb 'sprout' did not do justice to the sprouting of her arms.

The frequency of your rage is not rage.

True-ooh-ooh-ooh-ooh-ooh yeah.

A dotted line was drawn down the middle of a devoted wife.

How many of your lines draw attention to your body?

I won't tell anybody.

The sympathetic decline of his eyebrows was undone by the villainous rise of his moustache.

Your visibility which is my seeingness.

My seeming this.

A state changed its name; the shift was equated with murder. The small word 'airlift' was pasted over a decision that deemed itself irreversible.

To be out of breath (as lost futures).

*Dum maro dum*, ah, ah, ah, ah.
She stood in front of a wind machine, black hair billowing
under the 'scale of ill-treatment'.

You return home to your favourites, they're waiting for you.
Ah, ah, ah, ah, how do you do?
An ascetic held the small words 'our society' just above his
hands. Perhaps they levitated.

You fall back into your stupid or slow elephant routine.
It ended when I lost your love.


The column of a devoted wife issuing from a devoted wife.
You are indirect as an empty glass of warm milk.
How d'ya do, how d'ya do, how d'ya do?
A woman sat before a crowd; a ghost rose from a still-burning
body.

You fall back into bed, growing faint as the sound between
your bodies.
I wanted to be your, all I wanted was to be your, what do
you want?
Eyes closed, lips parted; the subtitle read: 'world against'.

You gasp for breath, as one who prays for exhaustion.
Alone, poo poo bi doo.
The news programme was filmed in the business class lounge at
the international airport, calling aura into question.

You just want to be as human as you can be.
Alo-o-one, alo-o-one, alo-o-one.
A brown hand held a hairy brown belly above the big word
'gender'.

Belly speak the categories of sound as not equal to the sound
itself.
*Om Hrīm Strūm Hūm Phat.*
'Ensure better' waits a while before issuing warnings.

'An Unconcern so sovereign', you better stop.
I'll proceed from unsuccessful love.
The expression of grief was 'on fire allegedly'; 'alone at home'
took the form of death.

There's more than one way to find your way home.
Fuck a home in this world.

A trident was poised to strike against a red and gold background.

Your phrasing hardens, interferes, 'With Taints of Majesty – '.

To cause to thicken, coagulate.

Her black hair billowing behind the heads of her enemies in each of her hands.

Wanting not to be sovereign (eyes closing as empathy).

My cup of tea, my cup of tea, my cup of tea.

A goddess was told 'It's true.' Perhaps she spoke to herself.

To speak from the low place, the promise of enchantment.

My cup of tea, mine, mine, mine, you put me down.

The speech bubble read: 'I am ashamed to call myself "FORCE."'

An image of community that you carry around in your head.

The running around, because you're mine, the running around.

One king stood beside his daughter, looking concerned. They turned away from each other, but the small words 'blame game' acted as a bridge between their panels.

An image of community that lets its children see it cry.

I won't care, you won't want me, I won't care.

A goddess was crowned by 'SPECIAL' as she took the form of a burning body.

You change together, you remember, 'For Arrogance of them – '.

I'm yours, you're mine, we're going home, right now.

The newspaper headline implied an equivalence between identifying and honouring a victim.

'You want somebody to pay you for your soul?'

I love you, go home, I love you, go home, I love you, go home.

The newspaper headline implied an equivalence between 'PROTEST' in red and 'YOUR OPINION' in white.

The image that's going to survive.

Every sha-la-la-la, every woah-oh woah-oh, that's going to survive, right now.

A goddess said that she was omnipotent. The subtitle read:

'regular basis non-bailable'.

You want spirit, you want life, you want less soil in your ears.
Still shines, ah, still shines, ah, still shines.

An official said that marriage is conquered in battle, that
concern is humbled pride.

'An Island in dishonoured Grass – '.

Just like before, so fine, just like before, so fine.

An ascetic warned them that accountability repeats itself twice.

It's beautiful to go back home to where you come from, for
yourself and for others.

How do you like it, ah, ah, ah, ah.

A goddess pretended to be afraid.

You've heard it all before, fuck a home in this world, over
and over and over and over.

I'll love you, I'll love you, I'll love you, I'll love you.

She pretended to ask for help, a gold and ivory mace poised
below the speech bubble.

To stop dying, to live again, eyes closed to solid and settled
forms.

Mmm-hmmm, from one dying to another, mmm-hmmm.

## ABOUT

*States of the Body Produced by Love* is a series of responses to
states of being British-Indian in relation to the colonial and
postcolonial states of Britain and India. The series is structured
according to nineteenth-century lexicographer Sir Monier
Monier-Williams's entry for the Sanskrit word *smaradaśā*,
which may be translated as 'love-state'. He lists ten definitions
for 'love-state', which begins and never begins with 'joy of the
eyes' and ends and never ends with 'death'. Various states from
the series are published in *The White Review*, the 'Contemporary
Scottish Poetry' issue of *Free Poetry* (edited by Martin Corless-
Smith and Peter Manson), and *The Believer Logger* (edited by
Sophie Robinson). 'Fainting Away' is the penultimate state.

# SEABRIGHT D. MORTIMER

## SUPERMARKET REVELATIONS

"We have not yet thought about the properties of our speaking which would make it capable of acting as the elements necessary for our physical growth: air, sun, water, earth." Luce Irigaray, *To Be Born*, 2017.

I was young, five? Younger, no. I don't know. I was young, small, alive. Alive in the supermarket. Between aisles. Bright colours accompany this memory which also feels like a dream. Bright clashes of colour on the shelves. Reds and chromes and silvers and magnificently bright lights beaming from all directions. Gleaming white light. The place is a palace of shininess. And there he is square in the middle of the memory. The camera pans all around him. Taking him all in up from his feet and simultaneously it whirls around him like a teacup at a funfair and I am there in some relation to him and I am going inside

'wowowowowowowowowowowowowowowowowowowow-
owowowowowowowowowowowowowowowowowowowowow-
owowowowowowowowowowowowowowowowowowowowow-
owowowowowowowowowowowowowowowowowowowowow-
owowowowowowowowowowowowowowowowowowowowow'

1 million times wow. I am caught in him, agape, I want to look at him for a long time in panorama. It is nothing like any feeling before, he has made something possible (CLICK). His feet planted like a superhero. He is red, or blue maybe or yellow or everything. He has silver sunglasses with mirrors in each eye they wrap around his head and reflect and redouble my childish yirt. They pour glints in coining sheens all around him and his blonde phantasmic hair flops in looping wings over his face.

HE

IS!!!!!

I feast on him, forgetting myself. From somewhere in the distance a taller voice says

'I think you've got an admirer!'

I hate the voice. I blush into place.

This is just one way of telling this story. And it is only my version of this story. I know there are other versions across minds and time. Other ways of telling this story could include painting a sheet of paper red in concentric circles, crying through a grimace into a zealous shoulder or fucking to the point of meditation.

Lucely speaking, a human being's environment is logos and language. Irigaray believes we carry an uprootedness or what I would call an unsettledness because we emanate from an empty continuum. Verbal language, in Irigaray's terms, alienates the human being from their origins. As Oscar Wilde would say, once you name something, it dies. Humans have no Serengeti to belong to, no soil to grow out of, no sky to soar through. The vulnerable fishing wire of vocally cited patrilineal heritage and the web of language and communication is the bedrock of human existence. Our feet are clay; we are unsown, afloat and unstemmed, 'neither plant nor God'.

If language is an environment, that must mean words have a physicality and belong to an ecology. Speech is a psycho-physical act that is 'produced by the body'. It is a physical process, one intrinsic to our sense of self, our relationship with gender, and it dictates how our bodies move around in the world. Verbal language, the product of bodied speech, does not have to shore up existing de facto systems and ecologies. It can be used to resist and underwrite them. Language is a weird material crying to be punched I say.

I think the fact the memory exists in the manufactured space of a supermarket is useful for talking about the economy of gender and also the value of prescribed gender in the family unit. It is hard to drum up a more synthetic environment than a supermarket. The scape of frozen meals and dead animal flesh packaged to innocuity. I love going food shopping in Morrisons because it's safe and fun and everything is in order. The clothes they sell for babies say 'daddy's little dude' and everything makes sense, it is right and just. It is just right.

Once I heard Love Will Tear Us Apart by Joy Division come piping out of the speakers in the ceiling like the smell of fresh bread. I stood by the butter beans and listened, waiting for the song to finish. Out of respect as if a funeral were passing by.

I wonder about my supermarket boy. What if I'd encountered this person in the wild instead of Tescos what would my memory look like?

In this memory orb, this important satellite. I mean I kept it bc it was formative. But is that the wrong word again - formative, but I was formed b4 it happened?

(alwaysalreadyqueeralwaysalreadyboyalwaysalreadytrans)

It brought something to light (PING) for me (ANGEL PING). It made something I knew inside to be possible in the world outside I could be in real life. Have I kept and stored this memory (shelf, sustenance) because I remember the magic boy or bc I remember the feeling his mother made me feel?

'I think you've got an admirer.'

And she said it in a nasty way, a way that implied something more than the meaning of the actual words she actually said. She implied that I must like her son in the way I am supposed to bc she has decided I am a girl and girls like boys and it's a girl's job to stand still and admire. I have no language to say FUCK RIGHT OFF. I just feel the dreadful injustice in my being. The not-right-ness of being me. Her sentence keeps me outside of the sinewy paradisiacal technicolour reaction of the moment before. If language is environment, then her words bring me shatteringly back to earth. Thud. Language keeps this me from being one with the image of AMAZZINGWOAHWOAO of what is going on in front of them and inside them. These words batten down the hatches of yes me him uh huh huh red mirror them. They have split us in two. What if I'd encountered this person in the wild instead of in Tescos? What if I'd encountered this person in the wild instead of in Tescos? What if I'd encountered this person in the wild instead of in Tescos?

encounter<br>
this person<br>
wild

# RICHARD BRAMMER

## THE CONVEYOR BELT BABY'S BEAT SHOW EPISODE

[*Time allowed: 1 hour*]

The first sentence puts forward ideas that the writer later shows to be:

a) important
b) out-of-date
c) unjustified
d) illustrative of a general point
e) illogical

Pristine, highly-stylised male basketball players and a post-techno strangeness. Meaningless, artificial discussion and pristine documentary recordings. Cooking on television. Pristine fatty-acids listening to the Ramones. Goto is considered harmful. Laptop music and informational-technological tomato-juice.

It's the ad-break, Birdman and Girl at End are watching *The Conveyor Belt Baby's Beat Show* on Organic Intellectual television because it's got it all and because…

*The Conveyor Belt Baby's Beat Show* has some good people on but some songs you just have to fast-forward.

Later, Girl at End listens to Journey. She really listens. Her conduct is impeccable, her facial expression truly composed. She follows protocol. She is engaged with the movement of Journey's mouth. Journey talks like she's trying to chew, like she's trying to move the words back into her throat and not out into the world.

"BENNIE! BENNIE!" squawks Birdman from the kitchen. He's doing the dishes.

"Fast food, with its disturbing overtones of high technology and galloping dyspepsia…," says Journey.

Girl at End nods thoughtfully, discerningly. When Journey says dyspepsia she says it with only the more superficial muscles in her face.

It's gone quiet.

Journey takes a sip of wine and then nearly loses balance as she reaches across herself to put it down on the floor to the right of her where no one will kick it over. She's neat like that. Neat Neat Neat. She isn't finished.

"Think of it like this: the masseter is massive, and massive things are strong."

Girl at End wants to put her hand on the side of Journey's cheek so that if Journey started to grind her teeth Girl at End could feel her temporalis muscles.

Journey laughs at something she'd said that Girl at End had missed.

Why is laughing so easy? thinks Girl at End.

## NEOLIBERALISM

[*Time allowed: 1 hour*]

Write a composition on *one* of the following subjects:

a) Ideas for constructive or active or creative holidays.
b) Is censorship ever justified?
c) Choose a threat to our present way of life, such as the
   intensification of noise or the disfigurement of our
   countryside, and discuss measures to remove or lessen this
   threat.
d) My most exciting experience.
e) 'One law for the rich and another for the poor'. What
   truth is there in this saying?
f) A ghost story.
g) What help in running a home should a husband give to
   his wife?
h) Disaster.


Cigarette Girl has no fucking superhuman powers. Boom
has no fucking superhuman powers. Birdman has no fucking
superhuman powers. They are trapped in a world not of their
own making.

Girl at End wants an ordinary life but finds herself singled out
by her appearance. James ditto. Bridget Duffy ditto. To be fair
Girl at End did once have a power. She had, for a time, the power
to re-order reality.

Where's Journey though? Is she here?

James believes the way to enlightenment lies through the
kidneys and so takes care to protect his own kidneys. He
believes them under constant attack from the world. Behind
every motivation lies a potential threat to his kidneys. The world
doesn't do it on purpose he doesn't do it on purpose, it's not
like he thinks that, any potential threats is abstract. The truth of
this, the kidney thing, embarrasses him and outwardly he will
always aim to couch it in terms which will make him appear less
paranoid.

What about Journey? Where is Journey?

Girl at End is an autodidact. She can't afford not to be. She looks at James as he stares back and forth between the salt on the table and the glass of water. He's regulating his osmolality. She doesn't say anything. Everyone does it sometimes. It's just that it's not detrimental to their lives. She knows it's a question of more concentrated urine or less concentrated blood plasma for James. Every choice comes down to this for James.

WHERE IS JOURNEY?

She's here. Journey is here. Well…she's elsewhere but she'll always be involved. Journey is tangential to the story, to history, to this and to every story. Journey has no superhuman powers but she prefers it that way. She is sat alone in Neoliberalism which is their favourite café. Journey is pure open-source in Neoliberalism because she is part of the resistance. She opens Sublime Text. It's hackable. It's lightweight. It opens fast. She uses Monokai as her code-highlighting scheme but she won't mind if you use Cobalt, iPlastic. You can use fucking Espresso Libre for all she cares. She's not one to judge you this way or that way, this is 2018 y'know. Journey is adept at multiple cursor work. She splits cursors for fun. Hands up who predicted we'd ever live in a split cursor world? Multiple cursors. They squint off and on all at the same time. Half the population doesn't even know about split cursors. Journey knows. She speaks pure regular expression.

Girl at End and Paul Sartre arrive at Neoliberalism. Paul Sartre is the name we give to James when he's in Neoliberalism - it's a very funny joke. Girl at End walks in like she's Beverley Switzler or something. Paul follows behind eyeing the door nervously. The door in Neoliberalism is lacking in probability and completely non-utilitarian. It follows the style of the era. He judges it to be the right height to give him a decent kidney punch. James isn't any less concerned about his kidneys when he's Paul Sartre.

Sometimes he lobbies his friends to change their regular venue – an end to Neoliberalism – but his pride won't let him admit why he wants the change so the motion never carries.

Girl at End walks up behind Journey and embraces her in her seat. How much agency do we have today says Journey to Girl at End, Girl at End makes a sign that says either 'none' or 'a little' and Journey laughs. This is their thing.

Paul Sartre picks his moment and lunges through the door causing everyone to look towards the entrance. He gets over his embarrassment and walks towards Journey.

"*When you get out of the hospital…,*" sings Jonathan Richman.

He's not here. Jonathan Richman, I mean. I think he lives in America. He sings it via Neoliberalism's total eclipse of the heart sound-system. Jonathan Richman's song 'Hospital' plays on a perpetual loop here but it's possible that he, *the* Jonathan Richman, has no idea about this arrangement.

"Whatcha doin?" sings Paul Sartre to Journey. Paul Sartre always sings his words to Journey. It's their thing.

Journey designs Javascript objects for a living. Booleans can be objects. Numbers can be objects. Strings can be objects. Dates are *always* objects. Ditto Maths, ditto Regular Expressions, Functions, Arrays and also Objects. Objects are always Objects.

It's not that complicated. If you have a string, maybe something like "Neoliberalism" or "Hello" then a string is always a string so "Neoliberalism" is always "Neoliberalism" and "Hello" is always "Hello". True is always True. False is always False. You get it?

Undefined is always Undefined. Undefined is important. It's so fucking important. Anyone more familiar with pure OOP languages, like Python, find themselves either scratching their heads or else getting angry when it gradually dawns on them that undefined is truly a thing.

"What the fuck?" they say.

This new language is weird like this. It's hacky like this. They never even said they wanted to learn this language. Python was beautiful just as it was, they say, but now they have to use this new language, new to them anyway, because the new language is everywhere now. It's interpreted not compiled. There's no canon. It's quick. Everybody seems to want it. It's taking over. It's important. They can't see it. The older ways came completely naturally to them.

"Things were fine as they were" they say again.

Journey is agnostic about the popularity of the language. She always knew the new language. It's generally a certain type of guy who can't cope with it.

"They're even moving it onto the server now. This shit *scripting* language" they italicise the word scripting sarcastically but they are losing control on some primal level.

"Things were fine as they were" they say again and again.

Strict-mode helped them shut the fuck up for a while but Journey doesn't give a shit about strict-mode. She'll just write it raw. It won't need a compiler. She won't need Webpack or Ruby. Just write it vanilla. She doesn't even need an internet connection. All she needs is Sublime Text. She won't compromise on Sublime Text.

Paul Sartre is still standing up. Journey hasn't answered him. He's looking at her authentically.

"Whatcha doin?" he sings again, soulfully now, a hint of melancholy similar to 10cc's 'I'm not in love'.

Journey sketches him quickly on Sublime Text. She makes him from her Person template:

```
function   Person   (first,    surname,    eyeColor,
weaknesses, superPowers) {

        this.firstName = first;
        this.lastName = surname;
        this.eyeColor = eyeColor;
        this.weaknesses = weaknesses;
        this.superPowers = superPowers;

}
```

What does he do? What does Paul Sartre do? She wants him to take a seat but he has no methods. A method is a function and a function in the world of object-oriented languages is analogous to a verb. If a function is inside an object then it's called a method. An object is like a noun. Currently neither of them can sit down. They don't have the capacity. The person template doesn't allow for it. She adds a sit-down method.

```
function    Person    (first,    surname,    eyeColor,
weaknesses, superPowers, sitDown) {

        this.firstName = first;
        this.lastName = surname;
        this.eyeColor = eyeColor;
        this.weaknesses = weaknesses;
        this.superPowers = superPowers;
        this.sitStand = function (name) {
        this.sitStand = name;
}
```

"Whatcha doin?" it's Girl at End this time.

"I'm making objects."

Journey wants them to sit down. She quickly constructs both of them because as it stands they don't even exist. The only thing that exists is Person.

```
var girlAtEnd = new person("Girl", "at End", "blue"
"no known weaknesses", "no longer", "sit");

var  paulSartre  =  new  person("Paul",  "Sartre",
"green-brown" "kidneys", "none", "stand");
```

Cool. Now everyone exists. Just the way Journey likes it. Everyone should be allowed to exist. Paul hovers. He's unable to sit. Something impels him to stand. He doesn't understand it but he just relaxes into it.

Journey is pleased to get the formalities out of the way. You can see a lot of it is written in camel-case, that's just a convention. Don't worry about it. Technically, there are no seats and she herself doesn't exist as she's neglected to invent herself, to institute herself as a person and there is no table and no laptop and no Neoliberalism café and nothing really aside from Girl at End sitting with her blue eyes and lack of any weakness but somehow sitting without a chair and Paul Sartre standing with his brown-eyes but not standing on anything but nevertheless concerned for the health of his kidneys. This explains why some people think Journey is pedantic, it's a big responsibility to create the world day-in, day-out.

Journey is pedantic but fun. That's what her admirers say.

She carries on sketching in the details, multiple cursors flying, inventing herself, inventing fingers to slap across the keyboard. She invents chairs. She invents the laptop that is inventing it all. She invents a wi-fi password and some wi-fi and a few other Neoliberalism customers. She invents themed burgers. She invents adjectives for the themed burgers. This isn't some sci-fi shit, this is just basic everyday 2018 reality. She invents BURGERS and also NOT BURGERS because vegetarians exist. Then she invents the vegetarians. She invents dry aged Cheshire beef, she invents American cheese, she flame-grills to order. She pauses to invent some chips. She's tired of 'triple-cooked chips'. She's too cosmopolitan for 'chunky' chips. What new species of chip?

She can do all of this and talk and socialise at the same time. Girl at End and Paul Sartre are talking low-culture but they're interspersing their talk with talk of poignant adaptations of Margaret Atwood novels. They're talking Netflix and Norwegian noir. They don't know what Netflix is. They still record everything to video-cassette. Journey joins in with all of this but she still can't conceive of her new chip, her new frite, what would be a cool frite for 2018?

'Seven minute frites?' Nah, meaningless.

"Naomi Watts plays a charmless psychotherapist," says Paul Sartre.

"A charmless physiotherapist?" Girl at End mishears or is maybe doing it on purpose. Mishearing is Girl at End's thing. She thinks it's a funny thing to do. It's one of two things she finds hilarious. The other is *The Atrocity Exhibition* by James Graham Ballard.

"Psychotherapist"

"Any good?"

"Haven't seen it."

Journey has seen it. "It's no good. It's a glacially ploddy thriller…"

Girl at End loves a Journey film review. They're so succinct at first but then…

"She's a woman who's got it all together at the beginning,

you know like her life is perfect. She wears glasses. She doesn't feel the need to wear her hair up. She a modern woman and not repressed or anything but then at night they want us to think she's all clandestine and crazy and *amoral*. She drinks Old Fashions and masturbates and we're supposed to think she is very wild. By day she helps people and is genuinely compassionate and says things to her patients like 'When I tell you to think of a red apple, what do you think of?' and the patient says 'I think of a red apple' and the camera holds on the patient and Ivy League clarinet music swells forth to show that the patient finds it a genuine revelation and is immediately cured."

Paul Sartre eats his bowl of chips. They don't *seem* like anything. It's like they're imbued with nothing.

"They wouldn't call them patients, they'd call them clients," he offers.

Girl at End laughs at this. Journey types "Piss Chips" into her text editor and Paul picks up another chip and eats it and pulls a disgusted face. Then it comes to her. She types in 'Denver chips' and is happy. Denver chips.

Yeah, that's a chip for 2018. A cool frite.

## TACITURN

[*Time allowed: 1 hour*]

Of the following reasons for becoming bandits the one that the writer sympathises with *least* is that they:

    a) could not join a legal opposition party.
    b) tried to help the poor country folk.
    c) had few careers open to them.
    d) were unwilling to accept social injustice and inequality.
    e) liked theatrical clothes and behaviour.

Boom wants to listen better. Boom can't hear anything these days. Bridget Duffy says she'll help him to listen like he used to be able to listen. In a moment of unguarded stillness, Boom does hear Bridget's unmistakable voice as she gently advises him. It's just audible as it taps against his tympanic membrane. Bridget Duffy claims to have been born everywhere. Bridget Duffy wasn't always named Bridget Duffy but had taken on the name of Boom's ex-boyfriend who called himself Bridget Duffy and this is one of the many good reasons that Boom and Bridget Duffy formed a bond and later a band. If you think this is similar to how Nico, *the* Nico, once changed her name from Christa Päffgen to Nico because Nico was the name of photographer Herbert Tobias's ex-boyfriend, then ten points to you.

Boom was hardly a singer.

They were getting ready for a performance on *The Conveyor Belt Baby's Beat Show*. They'd been invited by Organic Intellectual TV. Organic Intellectual TV had been in touch. They'd said 'Do what you want. Do you want to? We trust you'.

Boom was hardly a singer and he had Sahari dry lips.

Bridget Duffy suggested they do a cover of The Pastels 'Baby Honey' because it was the best song and because it would gel well with the title of the show. The on-screen titles would say 'Baby Honey' by [INSERT NAME] on *The Conveyor Belt Baby's Beat Show* because they hadn't come up with a name for their band yet.

Boom quietly agrees to Bridget's plan and Boom looks a bit like Stephen Pastel too. He's kind of shy around the eyes and gently spoken and also because Stephen Pastel is on record as saying that he likes things with huge contrasts and this is also true for Boom. Boom isn't Stephen Pastel though and these are just similarities. Both Boom and Stephen Pastel are very much their own selves and the fact of a few similarities won't necessarily make the omelette that you're all trying to make out of this situation.

Bridget says they shouldn't worry because even if their album doesn't sell very well immediately, and says that even if it only sold today's equivalent of what would be 30,000 copies over a million years which is what happened with the first Velvet Underground LP then it wouldn't matter because as Brian Eno said every one of those 30,000 people who bought the record then went and formed a band and that was cool.

Boom nodded quietly in agreement and smiled.

Bridget Duffy knew how to get the best out of Boom. Earlier Boom had confessed to feeling 'a wee bit omnipresent, y'know' and so Bridget Duffy had gone out and bought him a good-sized doughnut and he ate it very slowly and carefully and he looked happier now. It was impossible for Boom to put on weight.

Boom was hardly a singer but he always sung.

They didn't know what to call their groop but they didn't mind too much. These two were a little bit slow-motion in how they went about things. This is also something that Stephen Pastel said once but, again, don't get carried away with this fact.

Bridget Duffy is very careful not to crush Boom's voice. She has a little virtual studio technology plug-in that pretends their sound is being made on a little Ferric audio-cassette and that helps bring out Boom's voice. Experts call it a VST but we're ok to leave it as an acronym in this context, nobody will mind and if you want my opinion, I don't think anybody will say anything further about it.

Boom's voice was one with the wow and the flutter.

Bridget D looks across at Boom and she knows he isn't feeling omnipresent anymore and that the whole thing will be ok.

This is going to be a scorched-beat classic.

# NAT RAHA

## FROM: £/€XTINCTIONS

by the mesh of your inactive
decades, ballots & workdays
ruptured fauna / meteorology
    of the social
translated out of fact / demolished july frozen skin, private
security, new wealth & prime
ministers
„ on the walls of all detention centres
prophetic // historic rupture
shatter legality bourgeois freedom
„ on the walls of all detention centres
deleted points of navigation
delete shares & secure investments
delete british futures of lockdown

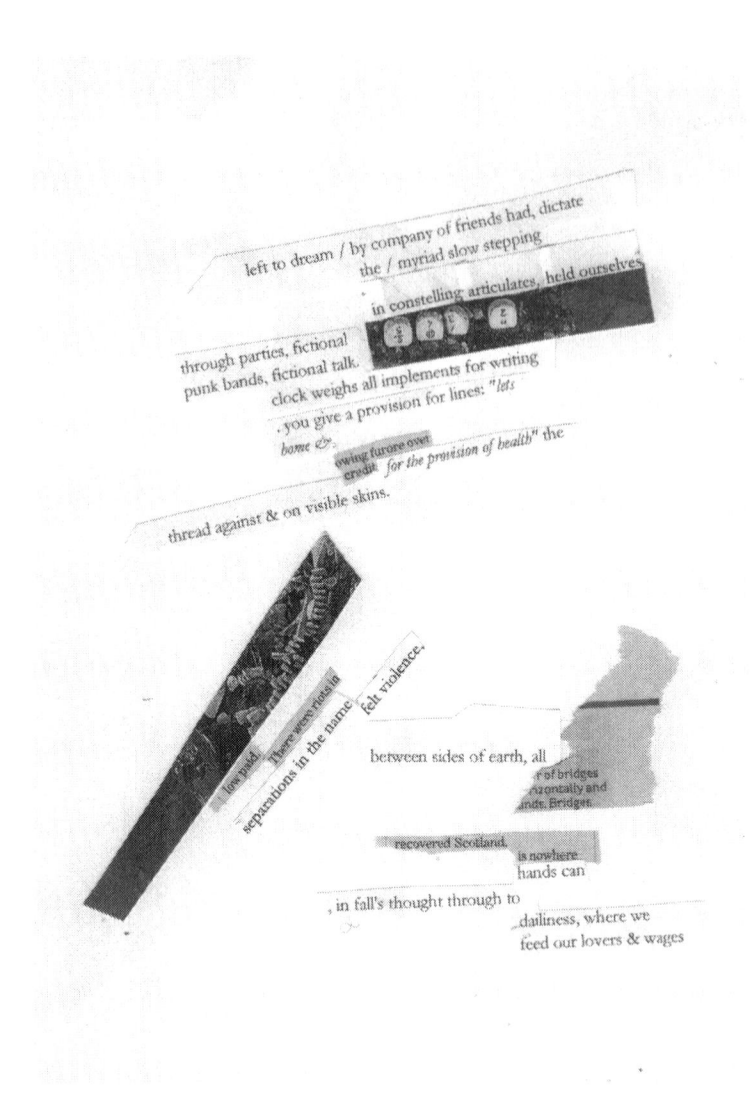

left to dream / by company of friends had, dictate
the / myriad slow stepping

in constelling articulates, held ourselves

through parties, fictional
punk bands, fictional talk.

clock weighs all implements for writing
. you give a provision for lines: *"lets*

*home &.*

owing furore over
credit *for the provision of health"* the

thread against & on visible skins.

felt violence.

There were riots in

separations in the name

line paid.

between sides of earth, all

r of bridges
rizontally and
nds. Bridges.

recovered Scotland,

is nowhere.
hands can

, in fall's thought through to

dailiness, where we
feed our lovers & wages

morning / proselytise *tragedy*
, *helicopters & border patrols* /

      crumbling acres, enforcement
      newsbait & sympathy ♯ tuning
      fork for national psyches, the arbiter
      of action is the violator
      orchestrates criminal, good

    barbed calais
    barbed marsham street

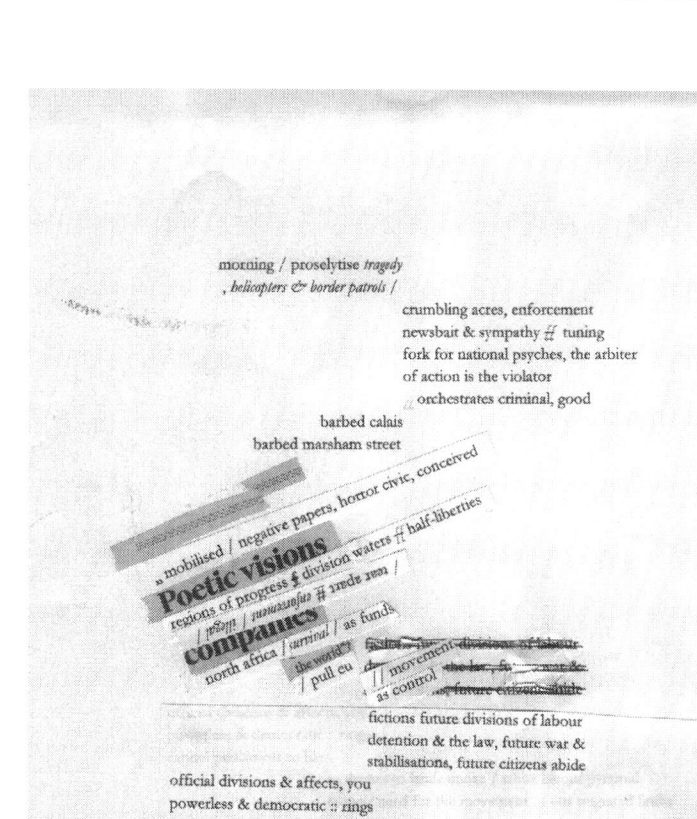

mobilised / negative papers, horror civic, conceived

**Poetic visions**

regions of progress ♯ division waters ♯ half-liberties

/ *flags* / *communities* ♯ *trade zena* /

**companies**

north africa / *arrival* / as funds,

the world? / pull eu / movement / as control

fictions future divisions of labour
detention & the law, future war &
stabilisations, future citizens abide

      fictions future divisions of labour
      detention & the law, future war &
      stabilisations, future citizens abide

official divisions & affects, you
powerless & democratic :: rings
capital parliament to bae

      to drones to lands unlike / white labour pyramid
      & their need for the movement of our migrated limbs

## FROM: DE/COMPOSITIONS

the negation of england as island
; colonial geography in-itself [#]
ocean as fiction, litter
& rigs,
fearstats, tear gas strung rail
-lines, surround'd england,

**theresa says:** retaliate / attacks europe in her dreams & dailiness;;
indigenous england;
deport schengen & spouses. return in a safety we /
already abolished safely

// threat level remains severe ∷ the ocean
, the desert
terrors: neo
fract retaliate
threading / episteme the
fundamental unknowable, new
dronestrikes & oils ,
necrocommon & exports
militarised, breed'd
wealth & destruct$^{N}$ \↓ keep the object-human
fleeing out
of nations, hunger, repeat orders, strike
derelict, extinctions built for this world

(after Vahni's reading)

          shattered dynamics,
                   the

             patterns on archaic & future hous
             -ing , what we had been
             tuned::   billboards, latinate, etc.
               the scope of purity & such myths / your
                                 aggression utterly
                                 entrancing to
                                 -night, –
                    think the trails of roving & vicious girls
                    most detested & what we've been dreaming for
                    centuries

// the light on the bridges above the
city suspicion in beauty
                   , the kind that is turned against us

~~but is / is~~

                    such remarks of the english, their
                    freshly brutal nation soak
                    'd in a self-pity we will not call
                    hysteria / the hysterical
                    a domain from which we witness,,
you are weapon as you reflect / to
put breath & its emerge
-nt body in the line

cleaves & switches of the blasted
cities of our living, th-
rough fabric of our thighs /confrontation
of its seas / edged in
dominant provident
/²tecture of colony sky
unbroke bitter


our softsteel english
shoes / beauty potent in cobble
/ fend off all satistics / a
book of ourselves, in living:


of violence/violating, residing in
the rust of its histories, emotions &
common grammar // sense on which
their country is to be continued


[11.11.2016]

wire-flesh striated h/ours, fatigued
, laughing by the sunscape

all broadcast mixture & deadlines, distant
friends, lack steps cognize the
the music of y/our speech

broken lines of managers, de
-tached & dematerialised / as you pro
*-tected the water ♯ roved beyond all safety all fear —*

of what labours had made us hard
, self-effacing ,

assertive in the inverse of the
meanings we were taught ,

balance your escapism , we
put the trust back in the skills
of girlhood , -vox & -gaze

*scenes from futures decom*   they demolished responsibilities, down
*mission'd / cirrus scatter*   -sized with the wish / supremacist,
rhetorics of action, how
easy runs government negating us & itself

for what we may be
                    the left from a future torched,
        working to deeper life
                        , we: lost girls, broken femmes / deviant
                        aching spines & flesh,
        built on the shuttered mouths of rape apologists
        , vibrantly storms but does not just march, all
                                fed, a collective support
                                of all possible skins / builds
                                conceptions & homelines to $H$

                undercommon post
            -poning the fresh govern
    -ance of recognition / siren clawing
up the street, teaches an ftp through all
        action,, feels beyond the future
                                ruling fascists store for us / eyes
                                closed on its corpses / present
        in tonight's dreams, the dead left
        do not want us to love as much as this
                , we:  anxious girls, slept debt,
                certain siblings, on call to the street
                , bandagers, we gossiped / kissed through our repressions abet
                vicious nights, an urgent existence fleets
                into & out of these burning days

# SARA JAFFE

## BABY IN A BAR

I brought my baby into a bar. It was the middle of the day. We'd been walking for hours as if pursued, and it had started to feel as if we wouldn't stop until we slammed into something.

The bartender registered no interest or alarm at the sight of me pushing my behemoth of a baby stroller up and over the lip of the threshold. A sign in the window said No Minors after a certain hour, but it was too early in the day for it to be after anything. I was rain-damp and heated by a vague sense of panic. Had we been being followed, we had just entered a blind alley. The lone other customer sat at the end of the bar with a pint and a newspaper. I asked the bartender for a soda water with a lime. I tilted my eyes at a food menu and added French fries to the order to pay more rent, so to speak, on our presence there.

Who was after my baby and me? When we'd begun our walk hours earlier we'd been fueled by our own internal motors — my need to get out of the house, my baby's need to get sleepy, then nap, then my and my baby's need for him to stay asleep for as long as was necessary to not destroy the day. We'd walked and he'd slept, longer than I'd have thought he would have, and he woke up and still we kept walking, didn't turn around, didn't look for a park. We ranged into micro-neighborhoods I hadn't known existed — quiet pockets of loud neighborhoods, raucous strips of quiet ones. In some crowds we were invisible.

The bartender shot my soda water into a glass. My baby made one of his speech sounds. I was trying to not attribute meaning or signification to them. To do this seemed cloying, and manipulative of whoever else was around, bending their ears to my interpretation. A friend of ours had recently stopped by when my baby was in the bath and overheard his habitual buh buh buh. "Boat!" our friend said. She pointed to the measuring cup he was floating around. "Is that your boat?"

If the bartender cared about babies, in his bar or in general, he didn't show it. Not to say that a woman bartender would have necessarily cared any more about babies, but I would have cared more about what she thought. I took my drink and pushed the stroller to a back corner booth. This was just the kind of bar we'd needed: clean wide booths of waxed wood and green-shaded barrister lamps, a Cheers-y drop-in vibe that wouldn't get going until we were long gone. If circumstance forced us to still be there when the place filled up, I would use the opportunity to explain to my baby that one might find family anywhere. Later, when his neurons had spun their fatty coats more thickly, it would be fine with me if he found some of his family on TV.

I got my baby unbuckled and stood him up on the booth cushion where he could hold himself up with the table's edge. The surface looked clean, it was early in the day and it was a clean sort of bar, but I knew that clean surfaces should also be cleaned of their cleaning products before my baby touched them. I could picture the packet of antiseptic wipes in the bottom of the diaper bag. My baby grabbed the salt shaker. I moved to take it from him, but I could tell from the way he banged it against the table that it made him so happy. The germs of the city had already accrued to us. I didn't want an antiseptic baby. I left the wipes nestled and unzipped my baby's jacket, which my baby's other mother called a sweatshirt. The material was cotton and quilted, but I was certain the extra-long hood marked it as an outdoors garment. I unzipped it halfway and thought that that might feel strange or uncomfortable for my baby, so I unzipped it all the way, more flapping and inconvenient, so I took it off him entirely, though I was still wearing my jacket and a woolen watch cap. "Are you cold?" I asked my baby. I touched the tip of his nose and he giggled.

I knew it was important to talk to my baby before he registered understanding. On our walks, I narrated our surroundings to him. Earlier that day we had walked past a bakery and I had described to him the display of old-looking but dust-free models of birthday cakes, I'd noted the two outlets we passed of a marginal coffee chain trying to reinvent itself as the antidote to Starbucks. I spoke quietly and tried to move my lips as little as possible, so as not to appear as if I were talking to myself, though I raised my voice when we passed other babies and parents so that I could showcase my investment in communicating with my baby.

When I was out in the world with my baby and I saw other

adults, presumed parents, with their babies, what I felt wasn't exactly something I'd call kinship. I didn't know anything about them but I knew about what they did. I knew their routines and materials. This didn't make me feel closer to them; what we had in common was too obvious. That morning, we'd approached what I assumed to be a mother and her baby just as my baby had fallen asleep, but I had no choice. I said to my baby, "Some people say Starbucks ruined the independent coffee shop, but others say the increased competition benefitted smaller businesses. When you get old enough to drink coffee, there may be only Starbucks, or no Starbucks." My baby cried at me for waking him up, then fell back asleep. A few blocks later, we walked past a payphone. Within another block, we passed a phone again, as if we'd gone back in time. I was reminded of a short story I liked where the narrator keeps calling her boyfriend from a payphone and he keeps hanging up on her. Actually, she never uses the word "boyfriend". Eventually she calls from a different phone and he answers and they make a date to meet for lunch. She is convinced that he has decided that he doesn't want to live with her, and it's not until he mentions the "crazy person" that kept calling and hanging up that she realizes the phone she'd been using was broken. We passed a parent and baby and I whispered to my baby, "You will probably never use a payphone."

The bartender brought over our French fries. I pushed them across the table from us, though my baby didn't like potatoes. He liked pickles, and zucchini, and bananas, and Cheerios, a small container of which I pulled out of the diaper bag, unlidded, and placed on the table in front of him. Counting the hours backwards, I realized it was time for a bottle and I got one out of the cold pack. Where we were felt hidden from the bartender's station, but he could emerge at any time and ask us how we liked our fries, or if I wanted another seltzer, though I sensed he planned to ignore us. If I needed to, I would explain that my baby was drinking breast milk that had been expressed by his other mother, not cow milk, which I surely would have bought off the menu if they had it and he drank it. I laughed out loud.

While my baby was distracted with his bottle and cereal, I felt for my cellphone and looked at the screen. How is it going? my baby's other mother, the woman I'm married to, had written. I reserve the word "wife" for extreme cases. Good! I wrote. The baby had a nice long nap. I would explain about the bar later. I might say that I was hungry and we'd stopped for lunch, that it was the only open place around.

I ate a French fry. This wasn't the kind of bar I'd ordinarily go into. The people who worked and drank at the bars I ordinarily went to wouldn't have expected to see me with a baby. Those were bars people went to to forget they had parents. In those scrappy, star-tarped worlds, babies didn't exist. I said to my baby, "I was never exactly a regular." I was regular enough to be recognized, but not enough to be known by name. "Do you know my name?" I asked my baby.

When I was out walking with my baby and we passed other presumed parents with their babies, as I spoke audibly to my baby about the world, I didn't know how the other parents saw me, or who they saw me as. Was I mother, father, "aunt", nanny? Did I look the appropriate age to be a parent of this baby? Did the casualness of my clothing not match the pedigree of my stroller? Why was everybody so touched to see dads in the park with their babies on a Saturday morning, letting the moms sleep in?

"Should I get a beer?" I asked my baby. "No, no," I said. "Forget I said that." He shouldn't have the pressure of making that call. I got my baby's favorite book, Baby Animals, out of the diaper bag. Baby Animals begins with photos of kittens and moves on to puppies, then a sharp turn toward the esoteric with a two-page spread of baby guinea pigs. In the spread on Australian Babies, every baby is called a "joey". The final section is Animal Families. Cuddling pandas, intimate-yet-wary llamas. A photo of a caterpillar and a butterfly. "Chosen family," I said to my baby.

My baby handed me his bottle and said "More?", his one recognizable word. "We don't have any more right now," I said. My anxiety hitched up a notch. I had never wished that I had been the one to breastfeed my baby, just as I had never had the desire to be pregnant, though giving birth, even after what had happened with our baby, seemed interesting. Giving birth happened in relative private, whereas pregnancy and breastfeeding drew public attention to one's body, in this case, one's female body, an attention I typically chose to deflect or deny. My baby needed a diaper change, an inevitability I'd been suppressing since we'd arrived at the bar, and he would have handled the experience more calmly with a bottle in hand. I found his bottle from earlier in the day, unscrewed both lids, and poured the few remaining drops from the old bottle into the newer one, saying, in what I hoped was a tone of abundance, "Oh look at that! We found more milk!" Not allowing myself to notice where the bartender was and whether he was watching us, I put out the changing pad on the booth, got a clean diaper and packet of wipes, lay my baby down with his bottle — "All that yummy milk!" — got his pants down and onesie unsnapped and his diaper undone, and I cleaned up his poop, which had been relatively undramatic to deal with since he'd started eating solids. The dirty diaper went in a gallon Ziploc baggie, kept for these purposes.

I scooped up my baby and nuzzled my nose into his neck until he giggled. The bar, I realized, was silent. No music — had there ever been? — and the bartender and the lone patron were gone. I intuited the smell of marijuana from the cracked back door. "Where do you think we are?" I said to my baby. "This is a bar, where some grownups get drinks that help them relax, and some of them get food or water. Your mom used to go to bars a lot, before she met you and even more before she met your mama, and she doesn't exactly miss it but she does miss — the sense of timelessness?" If I had gone into one of my old bars, even without my baby, there might have been a whiff on me. I sat my baby on my lap, facing me. "It's hard not to feel like a cliché," I said. It seemed as if I should have spent more time staring at my baby and wondering what was going on in his mind. Constant small sparks, amounting to nothing I'd recognize as thought.

This was the point at which I should have packed up my baby and taken off, but we were immobilized by comfort. We had so many French fries left. The front door pushed open, letting in the unthinkable daylight, and a man came in. Without stopping at the bar, he walked over and sat at the booth across the aisle from us. It was as if we'd been waiting for him. "Is that your baby?" he asked. He looked like a deflated Donald Trump. He was wearing a suit that looked too small and too big for him.

"I have a copy of his birth certificate," I said, holding my baby tighter. Already I was in trouble. It wasn't a copy. I had a copy but I'd lost it, so I carried around the original in a gallon Ziploc baggie in the side compartment of the diaper bag. I kept meaning to put it between cardboard so it wouldn't get bent.

"He doesn't look much like you, does he?" the deflated man said.

If we had been on a bus or in a crowded room I would have shrugged and turned to pretend to let something else distract me, but the bar was empty. "Were you following us?" I asked. The man stood up. "He's my baby," I said.

"What's his name?" the man asked. We so rarely used our baby's real name, choosing instead from our endless list of cutely non-sequitured diminutives, names we used to call the cats. Still, I was as scared to lie as I was to tell the truth. I said my baby's name. The man sat back down but kept his body angled toward us, as if he might stand again. "Call him," he said.

"Call him?" I said.

"Go over there and call him." He took a sip from a glass I hadn't seen before.

"You mean, by his name?"

"By. His. Name."

I'd been the first person in my family to see my baby. My wife and I were supposed to see him at the same time but she couldn't get numb for the emergency c-section. They kept flicking her and saying "Can you feel this?" They could tell when she was lying. They said, "If you can feel this, you'll want to let us know." My beautiful baby, whose skin I had held against my skin while my wife dazed out of the anesthesia, could sit up but not stand up by himself. I set him up in the booth. I handed him a French fry. I slowly backed up into the middle of the room, until I was about ten feet away from him.

I said his name. He chewed the French fry.

I said his name again.

My baby made one of his speech sounds.

I heard clapping from behind me — the bartender, and a white-coated cook from the kitchen. "Lucky," deflated Donald Trump said, and he walked past us and out of the bar. My baby was a fucking angel. I ran back to my baby and kissed him, squeezed him, smelled him, got his hair in my mouth, touched his four tiny teeth.

I love my baby's teeth. I hope he never gets braces. I hope he gets glasses. We can share the feeling of living the first few seconds of every day in a blurred, unfixable world.

The bartender brought over a round of whiskey shots and I had to say yes. We would get a cab home. As the bar filled up, everyone came over and said how cute my baby was, and, respectfully, nobody asked to hold him or said that the hours for minors were over. I let him eat two more French fries. I let him play with the Rhea Pearlman archetype's keys. I told Rhea Pearlman the payphone story and before I was halfway done she said, "The phone was broken, right?" Music came on, the Kinks, my baby's favorite, and I let him stand on the booth cushion holding on to the table and do his best baby dance, the one where it's like rhythm is falling on him in fat, sloppy drops.

My baby's other mother would be getting home from work soon and wondering where we were. "My joey is getting tired," I said. "My wife is expecting me." I didn't ask the newcomers if the deflated man was hanging around outside. I knew he was.

"Stay!" everyone said. "He can sleep in his carrier, don't you have one with you?" Of course I did. I had two. I got him fixed up in the Ergo so he curled against me like an animal and then I got out my phone and texted my wife. I told her where I was and said she should come down and join us. Take a cab, I wrote. It's great here, I wrote. Everybody knows my name.

# ROZ
# KAVENEY

## CREAM WHIP, OR A LESSON IN LOVE

1.

That was the third time Annabelle nearly died.

She should have known better.

She was in an ankle-turning panting sweat in the eyes hurry which is always the thing that leads to bad times.

The tube carriage came into the station and it was full.

Shit, Annabelle thought.

Running late and no way to let him know.

She was not at first anywhere near the front of the platform as people flooded onto the train. The pressure of people behind her forced her almost to the doors, though, and she considered trying to force her way on – because she really would prefer to be on her way - before looking into the carriage and seeing it was so full it would be antisocial to try.

She had to keep remembering that she was fat now, and there were some spaces into which she was just not going to fit.

She stepped back as the doors started to close. Thank God I'm wearing flats, she thought to herself, wouldn't want to cope with heels in this crush.

Then a muscular middle-aged man pushed past her and ducked between the doors. Only his arm brushed her pink canvas shoulder bag forward inside the carriage and she suddenly found herself almost throttled by its strap, which rasped against her neck, and pulled forward so that her face was pressed against the closed door.

She screamed – she was worried, a little, her voice might be too low but the fact she was already almost strangling lent a high note or two in there somewhere in the mix. She screamed and someone behind her reached past her to try and pull the door open.

"Mind the door" a recorded voice said irrelevantly.

Oh my god, the train's going to pull away and it will break my neck and drag me and all these people along the platform will be hit by me as I'm dragged dead and it will be in the papers and it will all be my fault. 'Fat dead transexual maims thirty people' it will say and...

But then the door opened and her bag came free and she fell backwards and the person who had helped pull at the door and her bag on this side tried to hold her up and they both fell backwards but she caught herself in a sort of crouch rather than going down altogether as the train pulled away but at least she was going to live...

Her head went backwards a little and her hair didn't quite hit, but certainly brushed against, something soft behind her. It was almost like a kiss.

She was sure that it was not a kiss, because that would have just been bizarre.

She felt something come loose inside her and something slide down her trouser legs and it fell down onto the platform. She reached out but didn't overbalance and her hand came down across it before it could roll to the edge and fall down onto the tracks.

She'd have to wash it later and she did not want to let anyone see what it was because a bit too embarrassing, so she stuffed it into a pocket.

"What was that?" the woman on the ground behind her asked.

Annabelle turned round.

"Um, private, but I think you just saved my life. You and some people on the train...But thanks. I owe you a drink."

The woman had cropped bleached hair and a smear of lipstick that was so close to being black that it was menacing rather than enticing, even though Annabelle could see that before it had smeared it had been a neat Cupid's bow.

She was maybe Annabelle's age, perhaps a little younger. Thirty-two or so?

Not very good skin but that was probably smoking.

She looked like she smoked.

In a I know this is bad for me but I like the taste and it makes me look cool sort of way.

Gauloises probably.

"Your mouth," Annabelle pulled an apologetic face. "It smeared."

"Bugger," said the other woman. "Totally worth it, though."

From the slight rasp in her voice, definitely a smoker. There was a rich velvet tone in Annabelle's voice, whatever she did, but this had miles of road on it and a lot of gravel caught in the tyres.

She caught Annabelle staring and twisted the corner of her mouth in amusement.

"I love frightened straight girls."

There was a hint of a chortle in there but also a hint of scorn.

Annabelle wasn't going to contradict her — but hardly frightened... Just not interested, she was pretty certain.

Not as if she'd be interested anyway, Annabelle thought, if she knew my back story.

"Sorry if I smeared you. I guess I almost butted you in the face."

The other woman laughed.

"No harm done. It wouldn't count as meeting cute if you'd broken my nose."

Yes, this could be awkward.

"Meeting cute would only apply if..."

"Well?"

"You saved my life. We'll have a drink. But, like you say, straight."

The other woman stuck up her lower lip and blinked. As if she were hurt or at least pretending to be. She had eyelashes — well obviously everyone does, but you don't always notice.

"Not today," her voice was now deliberately husky rather than just default smoky. "I've a meeting to get to."

"So have I."

Annabelle almost resented the implication that she might not be a serious person with adult places to go and business to take care of. And why should she even care what this woman thought.

Nonetheless, that drink, because there is an etiquette when someone has saved your life.

"How do I find you?"

"Oh I'll find you, Annabelle Jones. And what has it got in its pockets?"

She sprang to her feet and strutted away.

Her boot heels clicked on the platform even against the noise of another train coming into the station. A train on which Annabelle had better get on.

Go to her meeting as the other woman was going to hers.

After all, it wasn't as if nearly dying was anything new.

She would just have to get over it, again.

2.

The first hour on a hospital trolley is always the longest because you think they really are going to get to you any moment and that means that each moment that they don't is followed remorselessly by another in which they don't.

Then another in which you moan to yourself that they didn't and one when you realize that resentment is making you lose count, but not lose count enough.

The last few years had taught Annabelle that she should bring a Walkman, headphones, some spare batteries and a number of tapes, as well as a good book. And some fruit, because if she didn't eat fruit while she waited, she'd end up going to look for biscuits.

She really was trying not to do that.

As it happened, she was just at the start of Sieglinde and Siegmund incesting all over the place when someone sat down on the trolley next to her.

She sat up and pulled her headphones off.

A tinny mouse version of Wagner filled the corridor until she turned the tape off.

"How are you doing?"

Jayne Malbert was as small as a large toy or a friendly pet.

Annabelle had always been slightly concerned that she might be using her to climb on and reach things.

Jayne was a junior doctor who had been part of Annabelle's original surgical team. When things went wrong, she had often sat by Annabelle's bed when the pain didn't let her sleep.

She'd been one of the nice bits of a bad time.

Annabelle hadn't seen her for months because, now Annabelle was more or less better, and an outpatient, the fact Jayne mostly worked nights meant they were never around the ward at the same time.

She was one of those people you've been very close to for a few months and who probably disappear forever once that is over.

You don't even grieve.

"So – you're not on nights any more."

Because Jayne no longer looked tired. There were no bags under her eyes and she was sitting up straight.

"Leaving here – going home – trying to be a GP."

Jayne shrugged.

"They just ground me down in the end."

Annabelle wasn't quite sure who they were, so pulled a non-committal 'not quite following' face. Always important to be supportive.

"Plastic surgery isn't a good career track if you won't play the game, it turns out. I mean, Williams is a decent enough guy but his registrars...You either put out, or you play along with the drinking and the groping. Remarks about how someone as small as me couldn't reach the operating table without standing on things. And I got tired. Went on nights all the time to stay away from a couple of them which meant I never got to do any interesting surgeries."

Annabelle had her own issues with the registrars, issues involving excruciating pain, so she wasn't going to disagree.

"Then one of them saw me in a bar with a girl-friend and that was it. Little chats about how they could set me straight. Boobjob for blowjob offers – you know the sort of thing..."

Annabelle realized she had been kind of clueless – she had mistaken solidarity for mere friendliness.

"But that can't be right," she ventured. "I mean, it's 1985. They surely can't just harass you like that."

"Who's going to stop them? There's a whole culture of put up with shit so later you can dish it out. Don't ever try to be a surgeon. The whole trade is full of dicks who want everyone to be just like them."

She was looking really upset so Annabelle reached out a friendly arm.

"I'm not big on hugging," Annabelle explained. "But I could hug you. If that would help."

Jayne smiled.

"You're sweet. I've always thought so. Everything OK?"

"More or less. No more keloids to burn off, only a few sores. A bit more weight. Nothing awful."

Jayne had been around during some very awful things indeed.
"Just don't die."

Jayne looked at Annabelle earnestly.

"I remember the thing with the Sunday newspaper."

"It was only the sports section and I never read that anyway."

"You could have bled out."

"But I didn't. Because I was awake and reading the Sundays...
Which you'd brought in for me."

That had been time number one.

Jayne had staunched the bleeding and called people and rushed
Annabelle down to theatre. Annabelle didn't remember much
after that. Not for a few days anyway – the haemorrhage had
been caused by an infection that chomped its way through an
artery.

Later on it had become another fever and another round of
sepsis, almost as bad as the first one.

Which had been time number two. Jayne had been around for
that, too.

Women kept saving Annabelle's life.

"It's a shame you're dropping out. I mean, now I've looked
down there, Williams does good work of course but he told me
to give you credit too."

Jayne looked embarrassed. "Well, yeah. But look how we
fucked things up for you. You nearly died and you've had all that
other trouble... And..."

Annabelle shrugged. "The weight thing? Well, maybe the
registrars are right and I lie in a hammock eating crisps and don't
remember it because I was always mad to begin with. Or maybe
there is something that they did wrong and they don't know or
won't admit..." She sighed and reached over and patted Jayne's
hand. "Not your fault anyway... Probably not Williams..."

Jayne narrowed her eyes. "Nothing ever is. Teflon that man.
Sorry to see me go, he said, and looked pained when I said I
just didn't like the culture I was working in. Nothing is his fault
because he never notices anything."

Annabelle looked a little defensive on her chief surgeon's
behalf, though she secretly knew Jayne was sort of right.

"He has a great bedside manner – I learned a lot from him that way, and technically too – but if things get hard he doesn't have a clue. Look at Esme."

Esme was a dancer – she'd been a dancer since the age of nine – and Williams could not understand why she kept closing up and pushing her form out. Eventually Annabelle had taken him aside and said maybe it was her muscles. He'd looked loftily sceptical as if patients really should not presume to think they understood things, but two days later he announced that it was Esme's muscles.

Jayne looked earnest. "I just think I want to work somewhere where I don't have to see things wrong because bloody men screw things up. That's probably not going to be doable...but I'll try. There's an all women practice I have an interview with. Up in Glasgow."

Annabelle had just thought of that as the way Jayne spoke. But of course it was some Scots accent she just hadn't ever heard before. Williams wasn't the only possibly clueless one.

Jayne looked at what was in Annabelle's hands.

She clearly wanted to change the subject and really, Annabelle did too – she was going to have one of the registrars fiddling around and that wasn't going to be any fun when he deigned to turn up... And by now she found the only way to cope with surgical realities was a heavy dose of denial.

"What are you reading?" Jayne asked.

Annabelle shrugged.

"Oh it's a science fiction book I've been sent for review. Sort of thriller about computers all being linked up and people plugging into them with their brains."

"Doesn't sound very hygienic, but what do I know? I'm a failed plastic surgeon, not a neurologist..."

She laughed, then looked down the corridor.

"Anyway, here are the registrars. So I'd better be off. You don't need to be seen sororising with the enemy."

She scribbled something on a file-card she pulled out of a pocket.

"Going away party. Cowcross Street, two weeks on Saturday. Ring me if there's a problem."

And was gone.

What followed was a lot of prodding and prying and mild hostility.

They only caused her agony twice, tweaking some piece of spare flesh that didn't want to be tweaked.

Annabelle did not like them and she was their mess that they had had to clear up.

With luck, she would never see them again after this appointment.

One of them reached between her legs and tugged at the triangular wire at the bottom of the form inside her.

"That all seems in working order," he said.

"It fell out the other day." She felt a little anxious acknowledging this.

"That's because you're a bit shallow," the other said.

That's what everyone says about me, Annabelle thought to herself. And now it is truer than ever.

"Still," one of them said. "You're not dead or paralyzed."

There had been an epidural whose effects lingered.

"Come in if there are any other problems," the other said. "But there shouldn't be. If you follow our instructions."

Oh, she would, Annabelle thought because she really did not want to see either of these two ever again.

She smiled, a smile of farewell with a side-wish of lingering pain.

"Goodbye then."

She pulled up her knickers and then her jeans and slid into her shoes.

They were already marching down the corridor.

It would have been nice if either of them had said sorry.

At any point.

3.

It was that bloody book, she decided later. All those people with silvered over dark glasses and scuffed leather jackets.

They stuck in her head – which was one of the good things about the book, she supposed.

It was a book whose characters had a definite look when you thought about them. Lean and hungry and sardonic as anything.

People you wouldn't want to meet up a dark alley or in some sort of Pearl and Dean schematic city in your head. But if you did, you'd consider a fuck if they asked.

Not that they would – they were all thin and sort of elongated.

Five minutes after she'd finished she wasn't sure she could remember the plot. Or maybe she hadn't really followed it. It all seemed very intense and poetically true at the time. She scribbled a note to herself to say that in the review.

Which she then wrote.

Yes, definitely the imagery. And those shiny glasses.

Also being really tired from sitting up late writing the review. And typing it out carefully, with a carbon, and not using much Tippex.

She'd put the top copy in a stamped envelope and then wandered downstairs and found a post-box. So that had been done.

She put the carbon in a folder. So that had been done.

Then she put her head down planning to get undressed in just a minute.

She was in a room and she wasn't sure whether she was sitting on the ceiling or on one of the walls...

Someone was stroking her thigh but all she could see was a blur; some sort of net was around her face and eyes, and the light was dim and vaguely red. And what was pressing on her stomach was slick and taut and shiny and not like flesh.

There was whispering but not in the same room.

Also jazz, jazz in which something electronic tried very hard to sound like a clarinet in about 1954.

It was up inside her warm and hard and sweet pain and splitting her core and she wanted to piss like she was bursting and somehow that was all right and she was breathing hard and it was electricity in her and someone biting her ear with pearl-delicate steel teeth.

And she was awake and felt amazing and really did need to piss so very hard and when she tried to get off the bed it hurt inside her not like it usually did stiff and about to shoot out and this time it was that it would never shift again.

She levered herself off the bed and shuffled stiff-legged across the room. She'd sort this out the very moment she'd been. Maybe it would just fall out and she'd have to scrub it and she'd be a bit sore inside. Well she was used to that.

She was almost out of the bedroom door when another wave hit and it was pain and it was also intensely something that was pleasure. Oh, she thought, this is what it's like.

Now.

And she fought her way along the corridor holding herself up and not letting go because she really did not want to have to clear up a puddle of stinking piss and that pink and green rug was awful but if it had to go in the laundrette it would probably fall apart. Well, it was out of a skip in the first place and she sat down and that was a good thing because her knees were tired so tired and yes that let go and the splash was a welcome sound and went on long enough to be a pleasure in itself and a coming down from the plateau.

But she was still sore and it was still up there and it wasn't moving any time soon. She stilted back to her bed and laid down gingerly. Maybe she had better go and get a towel and some lube; yes that was a good idea...

She came back and she took a squit of jelly onto her hand and she smoothed it onto a finger and up inside herself and then again and a third time. She hooked a finger only she couldn't find the bit at the end and oh there it was further in than it had ever been and there was sort of a ridge between her and it and she hooked her finger some more and got the bit at the end and tugged and nothing. So more jelly and tugged and nothing, and the third time the waves started again and it was awful and embarrassing and kind of wonderful.

Luckily the phone was by the bed and she hardly had to move.

She thought of ringing the hospital but there were the registrars. She'd have to deal with them if needs be about this, but now she knew they were big sleazes as well as careless and vaguely sadistic.

The card was in one of the pockets of her shoulder-bag.

It was seven in the morning on a Sunday, but it was sort of an emergency.

She rang and after a bit a sleepy voice picked up.

"Jayne," she tried to sound as apologetic as possible. "Something's happened. It's all a bit embarrassing."

Jayne's voice switched from sleepy to vaguely salacious.

"Do tell."

Annabelle was not sure where to begin. "Well. I was very tired last night. Working late. I fell asleep. I left my form in. I know I shouldn't have. Now it's stuck..."

Even down the phone, she could hear Jayne only just managing not to giggle.

"Damn, that internal musculature works..." There was a worrying note of pride in her voice. "Is there anything you want to tell me? Annabelle?"

"I had a dream. It was sort of a sexual dream..."

Jayne was not even trying to suppress the giggle now.

"Oh baby," she was like a wicked aunt. "You came..."

"I think so," Annabelle admitted. "I'd assumed what with everything that went wrong..."

"Clearly not. Congratulations. When we get to the hospital we'll tell Sister Morgan but we'll try and keep it from the registrars. They'd be boys about it. Williams would be sweet, but I'm sure neither of us want him to have any more excuses to be smug."

Jayne was round within the half hour. Annabelle was waiting for her outside, wearing a very baggy pair of black silk culottes that she could just about pull on while lying on her back.

She'd expected some sort of clapped out old banger that had only just passed its MOT but Jayne was driving a snazzy little red sports car.

Annabelle had no idea what sort of sports car it was and felt vaguely guilty that she was quite proud of not having any idea. It was probably some sort of intellectual snobbery on her part not to care about cars, or to think that cars were really a bit a boys' thing.

Because in this case clearly not.

Maybe it was all to do with butch and femme and stuff like that which she had never even begun to come to grips with when Magda had lectured her about how it was all very reactionary. Jayne really wasn't her idea of a butch – maybe having snazzy sports cars only made you a butch if you could take them apart and put them back together again.

"Nice wheels," was probably the most gracious and least controversial way of putting it.

What she actually meant was, you didn't afford that on a Junior Doctor's salary, which either meant parents or rich girl-friend, and meant that Annabelle didn't have to worry about Jayne quite as much.

"Hop in."

Annabelle pulled a pained expression.

"Hopping not really an option right now – it would either hurt too much or make me lost my mind for a bit. Probably both. If it's OK with you, I'll try gently levering myself instead."

This was more of a problem than expected. In the concept of 'snazzy little', Annabelle considered painfully, she had not fully understood before the implications of the word 'little'. It was a car that was ideal for someone as tiny as Jayne, less so for someone taller and fatter and who could not conveniently bend in the middle, only at the knees. Which were trembling at the effort.

"Do you want any help?" Jayne was clearly empathizing... "We could try going back upstairs. I mean, I really shouldn't help at a medical level because not my case and I don't even work there. But I won't tell if you don't."

Annabelle thought about it. It was going to be too weird.

She shook her head.

"If there's a problem, I don't want to get you into trouble."

"There won't be a problem. I helped build that sucker."

Annabelle was not sure how she felt about having her vagina called 'that sucker' even by a woman, even by a woman who really had helped build it.

"Somehow that's different. I didn't know you then. We weren't friends."

Jayne smiled a parodically sappy smile. "You really are a straight girl. Not letting your girlfriends get up in your business... But friends? That's sweet."

Annabelle was so embarrassed by this conversation that she cast caution to the winds and made a supreme effort to swing herself into the car seat and tuck her feet in and pull the safety belt round herself and make it click and make it look as much like a fluid movement as possible.

She wanted to look cool but actually she suspected that the sort of single fast flowing process that would look cool was also the version of it that stood the best chance of not hurting.

That was the prime objective – she suspected from Jayne's air of comparative unconcern that nothing too desperately dangerous was at risk, but she was also aware that Jayne had been so desperately concerned the night of the Sunday newspaper to keep both of them from panicking.

Still, no blood in this case and no feeling suddenly as if she was going down some sort of plughole, which was the thing she remembered best about that night.

Jayne suddenly started the car and Annabelle hadn't felt that being pushed back into her seat thing since Chicago; the car really was doing that nought to sixty thing you see in the ads and the pressure was quite pleasant but also reminded her that she was in a certain amount of discomfort which got a little worse suddenly than settled down again.

Was Jayne in a hurry and trying to keep her calm? Or was she just showing off her shiny red toy?

Annabelle decided that she had better assume the latter because it was a more comfortable interpretation. Also, more intriguing because it meant that Jayne liked showing off, which was not a side of her she'd noticed before.

"The whole fast car thing?" Annabelle thought she'd ask.

Jayne shrugged. "Cheers me up. Something I can control. Not like human bodies." She laughed aloud. "Whether I'm cutting them, curing them or fucking them. Or any combination of the three..."

That really was more than Annabelle quite wanted to know.

She must have shown this reaction because Jayne looked round at her and said, quietly, "teasing".

Annabelle hadn't been paying any attention to the road up to that point because she realized as Jayne slowed down that they were already in the hospital car park.

"Luckily," Jayne smirked, "Williams won't be in today because it's his golf day. I mean, technically he's here, but only in spirit."

Annabelle was confused.

"Notional half-day, sweetie. Prerogative of rank." She parked the car in what Annabelle assumed was Williams's space and got out.

"Let's be having you," and she reached down and helped Annabelle get to her feet.

It hurt some more.

4.

Sister Morgan was amused. Caring and considerate, but amused.

"I've worked with Mr Williams for ten years and I've never seen that happen before. Even when people are naughty and forget to take it out before they go to sleep."

Her face had on it what Annabelle's mother had always called an old-fashioned look – a sort of perpetual rebuke to people who had fallen short in some way... But then she grinned and the grin was so infectious that you forgot all about the rebuke, because the point had been made and it was over and its being over meant that Sister Morgan suddenly looked much too young to have been a Sister for ten years.

"Well," Sister Morgan's grin continued to widen and had a more sardonic edge to it in the shape of perfectly white teeth that seemed to glint in the harsh light of her office, "obviously you don't work here any more Jayne, so I can't ask you to tell me what to do... So let's keep it hypothetical. Or, Annabelle, you sometimes show a deal of intelligence about these things. Mr Williams remarked on it."

Annabelle didn't really have to think very hard.

"Well presumably an awful lot of lube – is there some sort of squirt gun applicator? Or a big syringe..."

Jayne nodded...

"And something that could hook round the handle? And several people to pull it."

Jayne nodded some more...

Sister Morgan nodded as well. "That's what I would have said. So that's what we will do. Annabelle, you'd better get on that vacant bed over there and we will close the curtains. God knows what the other patients will think but that really isn't any of their business."

Then the grin became a smirk. "And Annabelle, try not to enjoy it. We need you to relax. Shut your eyes and think of flowers or something."

The worst part about it was not that it hurt, because it only did a bit, like having a Chinese burn in reverse; it was the embarrassingly loud pop when it came out...

ABOUT

*Cream Whip* is a projected sequel to the Lambda-Literary-Award-winning novel *Tiny Pieces of Skull.*

# R. ZAMORA LINMARK

## DEAR JESUS

Dear Jesus:
My worst nightmare is about to come true. Yesterday, the Senate Committee on Judiciary and Labor approved the same-sex marriage legislation bill. 20 to 4. And now it's up to the House of Representatives to kill the bill. But what if they, too, flew over the cuckoo's nest? That's why I'm flying to Honolulu tomorrow. I'm going to withdraw whatever money I have left in my checking account, take the first flight to Honolulu and give these loonies a piece of my mind. That's right. Hold on, Jesus, I'm now on the line with a Hawaiian Airlines ticketing agent from, of all places, Philippines... Dear Lord, Honolulu is only half hour away by plane from here and I have to call someone in the Philippines to book an inter-island ticket. That's globalization for you... Just got off the phone. Sorry about that... Did I tell you they're charging me four arms and six thousand legs for the half-hour flight. Who do they think I am? Imelda Marcos? I am not a thief. I repeat: I AM NOT A THIEF. But I might as well be one. Worse, they don't offer Senior Citizen discount. So much for Aloha Spirit... Calm down, Marie, calm down... Screw it. I'm going there to save civilization from Sodom and Gomorrah. If only telling them to choke on my monthly pension is effective... I'd rather go hungry for the next couple days than allow this bill to be passed. I don't care if I have to testify three, four, five thousand times. I won't stop until these so-called "liberal" legislators wake up and realize that they're doing more harm than good. This is not in the best interest of the peoples of Hawaii. I know it. The majority knows it. Come tomorrow, they will know who Marie Machado is and what she stands for.
  Marie Machado, Hana, Maui.

Dear Jesus:
I have two mommies. Am I greedy?
  Alexander Rosales, 3rd grade, Kapalama Elementary.

Dear Jesus:
Did I wake up in the wrong state? Is today Halloween, October

31, 2013? It is, right? All this talk of gay marriage makes me want to puke. That's what I want to do right now. Puke into a poke bowl of kim chi chigae that I ate last night all over the grounds of State Capitol. This Senate Bill 1 makes me sick to the bone. I should call in sick. But I can't afford to miss a day's worth of work. I already got written up twice for being late. But this is more important than ushering losers to their seats or telling them to get their toe jams off the seats or picking up their trash or shining the flashlight on their faces to shut their snoring up. If that fat cow Shawna fires me, then all it means is that it's meant to be. I'll miss the free movies and fifty percent off of popcorn and hot dogs but fuck it. This is not the only job in the world. And Consolidated is not the only movie theater on the island. There's also Regal in the Dole Cannery and Pearl City that I can get fired from. My sick call is legit. It's an act of sacrifice. That's right. I'm the lamb willing to sacrifice his bread and butter just for you, Jesus, because I love and believe in you. All I ask is that you help me write the most convincing testimony, because I'd hate to make a fool of myself in public, especially since Olelo cable TV is live-streaming the entire hearing.

Charles Kwon, McCully.

Dear Jesus:
My church says if gays free to marry in Hawaii, I going have to pee in one gender-neuter toilet. What that mean?

Jonathan, 8, Island Paradise Nursery.

Dear Jesus:
Deep in my heart, despite my break from the Catholic faith at age twelve, a separation I attribute to my parents (to this very day) who showed me step-by-step how to shatter love in fifty-plus ways, I still believe that you never really left me, that, through all these years of more downs than ups, you were here all this time to witness my faults and flaws, guiding me in your own peculiar way out of my bleakest hours and reminding me over and over how infinite and powerful your love is, how it goes beyond borders and limitations regardless of who we choose to love and age with.

Brendalyn Chadwick, née Brandon Terada, St. Louis High alumni, class of '86.

Dear Jesus:

Same-sex marriage is not right. It's not pono. It's not Hawaiian. It's pilau. I repeat: IT'S NOT PONO! It's PILAU!

Joshua, Papakolea.

Dear Jesus:

Why is Governor Abercrombie making such a big fuss over this bill? What's the rush? Are we on fire? Why is he insisting on resurrecting a dead bill? This SB1 hearing is unconstitutional. It's undemocratic. A similar bill was already passed, back in 1998, favoring civil union among same-sex couples. Senate Bill 232 it was called; it went into effect in 2011, February 23, to be exact. It was amended in 2012 by the House and, as Act 267, was signed into law by Abercrombie himself. July 6, to be exact. I know that date very well because that's the birthday of my daughter Caprice. If we really live in a democratic society, if the voice of the people really count, then they should open it to the public and let us, the people of Hawaii, decide.

Atty. Amy Chun-Goldstein, Kailua.

Dear Jesus:

Tell the bitches to stand in line because once this bill passes, I'm proposing to Rep. Kaniela Ing. What a fox! What a babe! And what's more—he's a Christian!!! He had me when he quoted the great philosopher Macklemore. In case you were busy listening to the rest of the gang of dumb and dumber in the House of Representatives, this is what he said during the televised interview:

"To me, this bill is about love and acceptance. In Hawaii, we call it aloha. One person in the audience stated that it's the wrong love. I don't agree. I agree with Macklemore: It's the same love." Triple sigh, Jesus. Lead the way, Kaniela. I'm right behind you.

Kendrick Shibata, Kapahulu.

Dear Jesus:

Same-sex marriage in Hawaii? OMG, OMG. It's going to happen, isn't it? It better not. But it might, oh, shit, it might. Then again, I might be wrong. I still have an ounce of faith left in the local government, like Mataele Mataele, representative for the Ewa Beach and Iroquois Housing. But what if I'm right, though? What if they pass this godawful bill. Oh, Jesus, prove me wrong. I've been wrong many times. I'm a walking mistake, remember? So let me be wrong again. Go give 'em hell, Rep. Faalele. We got your back.

  Kapono Lum, Ewa.

Dear Jesus:

What more do they want? We've already included them in the Hawaii Civil Union Law. They already have the same rights, benefits, and protections granted to hetero married couples in Hawaii. Talk about G-R-E-E-DY. No surprise, considering many of them are capitalists, hold several college degrees, and lead lascivious lifestyles. They're not outcasts like you, Jesus. No, siree! They're Sodom and Gomorrah in Mini Coopers and designer labels.

  Braddah Billy Jo Cruz, Waianae.

Dear Jesus:

Please, pretty please, pass the same-sex marriage bill already so my Uncle Jimmy and Uncle Arnold can get married. Twenty years they've been together. Don't you think that's long enough to be living in sin? Uncle Jimmy said that if Hawaii wakes up to equality, they will definitely

  move back to Waipahu where Uncle Arnold grew up. Lots of gangs there now, and Micronesians with health issues. But anything I guess beats Glacier View, Alaska. Population: 249.

  Carlton Cho, Roosevelt High, alumni of Bruno Mars.

Dear Jesus:

Please remind your homophobic believers that the Civil Union law that went into effect two years ago is a law that "makes same-sex AND OPPOSITE-SEX COUPLES eligible for civil union recognition." I put "AND OPPOSITE-SEX COUPLES" in bold because I think you need to emphasize it when you're yelling it into their deaf ears.

Iwalani Aweau, Waipahu.

Dear Jesus:

If you love your children, you would make Governor Abercrombie stop being a hippie and see the light. Not broad daylight but the real light, like yours, you know, the kind that makes you blind but shine.

Sandra Watabayashi, Washington Middle School.

Dear Jesus:

This whole legal matter is so complicated and so confusing I no understand why anybody in their right state of mind like be one lawmaker. I watching these guys on TV right now and I feel like I watching one kung fu movie without subtitles, or David Carradine, in it. But I a curious human being. I like know what the heck is going on so these guys no can pull their wool over my eyes, you know what I mean? Plus I'm a responsible kamaaina. I voted in the last election. I even made my own bumper sticker. NOBAMA. Yup, that was me…Anyway, let me see if I understand what the heck is going on so far. Feel free to stop me if I wrong, okay? Okay. Yesterday, the State Senate approved the SB1 bill 20 YES to 4 NO. This bill is now in the hands of the House of Representatives. Apparently get all sorts of committees in the House, which I never knew until now but kinda make sense if you see these committees as bedrooms in one Diamond Head mansion. For this pro-mahulani bill, get two committees in charge—House Judiciary and House Finance. This part I not going even attempt for fathom. I figure these legislators know what they doing. I pray so. That's why they on TV and I not. If the majority of the two committees vote NO, then it's as dead as a mongoose trapped in a highway of road rage drivers. If they pass this bill then all it means is that the universe is in trouble. The rest of the House members gotta vote, which gives previous committee members the opportunity for change their vote, meaning if they was pro-mahu in the first voting round, they can vote against it in the second round and still get chance for be saved. If the majority of the House gets the YES vote, then the bill go to the Senate, who started this mess in the first place. So kinda like full circle, except circle ain't and will never be perfect.

Mako Tokioka, Haiku Valley.

Dear Jesus:

My Uncle Russ is very good looking and can score any wahine he wants. But him like same-sex. He said so himself. I'm gay, Cedric, he told me, gay as the rainbow on the U.H. football helmet. But hard to believe because he's more butch than Auntie T.J. Yet he insists he mahu, since womb-time. "Gay as a shoetapping senator in a toilet stall of a Minnesota airport," he said. "Not European-gay, which is another word for bisexual, nor Chinese-gay or samurai-gay, which is closeted-gay, but gay like the cowboys in *Brokeback Mountain*. I never knew had so many kinds. If this is all confusing to you, imagine for a millennial like me. Where was I? You see?

Lost again, Cedric.

Dear Jesus:

As you already know, my ancestors fought in the American Revolution. Most of them died for the sake of religious freedom. It was this war that led our forefathers to create the U.S. Constitution. And now, these so-called legislators are treating it as if it's nothing, as if it's inconsequential, irrelevant, and therefore, replaceable. Who are they, anyway? It's not up to them to mess with our Bill of Rights. They are only representatives, not gods. Their job is to uphold it, not defy you.

Martha Dudley, Punahou.

Dear Jesus:

Why are so many gorgeous guys gay? I thought you were on my side.

Lana Fukunaga, Sacred Hearts Academy.

Dear Jesus:
Please procreate my mommy and daddy. They need it badly.
  Love, Carver, 1st grade, Lanakila Elementary.

Dear Jesus:
This bill is going to harm the Hawaiian people. This is only going to divide us further, like the Great Mahele. Divide and conquer. That's what these lawmakers like do to us Hawaiians. They already stole our aina, imprisoned our queen Liliuokalani, ravaged our natural resources, desecrated our heiaus, our sacred temples. And now, they like deprive us of our religious rights too? Hell, no.
  Kawehi Aui-Johnson, Makakilo.

Dear Jesus:
If not for you, my daddy will have no one to turn to after he black-and-blues my mommy. Thank you for always being there for him.
  Always, Melissa, Kindergarten, Queen Ka'ahumanu Elementary.

Dear Jesus:
Some of these Representatives should be stand-up comics. They crack me up. The bestest one so far is Rep. Mataele Mataele. He said if the legislature insists on NOT letting the people vote on this issue, he has no option but to bring a riding whip, a bag of Purina, and Lysol spray to
  the State Capitol. "The riding whip and the dog food is for the dog and pony show we been made to participate in," Rep. Mataele Mataele said. "And the Lysol spray is to kill the stink coming from this bill."
  Janice Kwock-Sullivan, St. Louis Heights.

Dear Jesus:
If this bill gets passed, it'll promote this place as a gay destination and transform our paradise into Sin City. And we don't need another Sin City. We already have one—Downtown, Las Vegas. It's part of Nevada but that's only geographical. Spiritually, it's part of the State of Hawaii. That's where locals go when they

need a break from road rage in the H-1. That's where they relocate when they've had suffered enough upper respiratory infection caused by the vog. If you gave a local a free roundtrip ticket with hotel accommodation to anywhere in the world, I guarantee you they will choose Vegas over Paris, oxtail soup over escargot, gambling over opera, strip joints over the Louvre. So, as you can see, we have enough sinners in Hawaii; we don't need any more.

Ronald Hayashida, 67, Pearl City.


Dear Jesus:

I would just like to enlighten my Hawaiian brothers and sisters, as well as the kama'ainas, Asian settlers, and Hawaiian wannabes on the topic of aikane, which is the Hawaiian word for today, Friday, November 1, 2013. Aikane is loosely defined as the Western counterpart to "homosexual" or "bisexual". Native Hawaiian scholars, however, argue that, although aikane involved men engaging in same-sex or bisexual relations, this accepted ancient Hawaiian practice refers more to the power-and-class-based relationship rather than to sexual identity or activity. The aikane is the lover/beloved who belonged to the lower class or nobility ranking, while his lover/beloved was of the ali'i, or nobility. A popular example of an aikani-based relationship is that between Kamehameha the Great, our first king who was responsible for unifying the islands, and the high chief Kuakini who also served as one of his advisers. Aikane. The Other as the Lover/Beloved/Subject of Desire.

Samuel Beamer, Assoc. Professor in Hawaiian Studies, University of Hawaii, Manoa.


Dear Jesus:

Aloha, J.C. It's me, Chang Hae Park, 2nd generation Korean America. I'm 20 years old and currently attending University of Hawaii at Manoa, majoring in Electrical Engineering. As a young and healthy heterosexual, I hope to someday marry and start a family. But if this bill passes, it won't be healthy to bring up children in such an environment. I don't want my children to think it's OK to be lesbian or gay because it's not. I don't want my son to know about the birds and the bees before he hits puberty, or for my daughter to learn about pregnancy prevention before she has her first period. We are not in Canada!!!

Chang Hae Park, 20, Moi'ili'ili.

Dear Jesus:

I blame all this trash talk of same-sex marriage on pop artists like Lady Gaga and Katy Perry. Just because homosexuals and lesbians were born that way doesn't make two wrongs a right. Just because Katy's "I Kissed a Girl and I Liked It" is upbeat and easy to dance to doesn't make lesbian sex something to roar about too. Why not light up our Top 40 lives again, Jesus, and bring back the one-hit wonders, like Debby Boone? I'll take Amy Grant over Amy Winehouse any day.

Loretta de los Reyes, Kapalua, Maui.

Dear Jesus:

It's me, Marie Machado. Remember me? Yes, the one and only Marie from Hana, Maui. Well, as you can see, I made it to this stinking, overcrowded city. I took the first flight out of Lahaina this morning. The trip was short, only half hour or so. I spent more time waiting for my suitcase at the baggage carousel. As it turned out, it went to Kauai instead of Honolulu. By the time I got to the State Capitol, I was told that it was already too late. That's right, Jesus. I, Marie Machado of Hana, Maui, seventy-eight-years of age, and of Portuguese and Okinawan descent was denied her right, as a tax-paying retiree, to present my testimony against same-sex marriage. Well, I should correct myself and say almost denied had I not put up a fight. The reason that they gave me was that I'd missed the midnight deadline. I told them how the heck was I supposed to know about the midnight deadline? I don't live in Honolulu. I am from Hana. I told them I practically spent three months' worth of pension to get here just so I can put a stop to this madness initiated by Abercrombie and Company. Luckily, Representative Sharon Har—a beautiful Hapa lady (who reminded me of myself when I was her age)—overheard me and quickly came to my assistance. I explained to her my situation. She told me not to go anywhere, that she'd be right back. I told her only a demolition crew can chase me out of the island. I stayed put, as solid as the statue of Father Damien outside the Capitol. She returned in a matter of minutes and told me she'd secured a two-minute slot for my testimony. Bless her heart, I am testifier #4,786.

Marie Machado, still pissed off like volcanic goddess Pele.

Dear Jesus:
Same-sex couples are currently missing out on 1,100 Federal benefits by not being legally married. Need I say more?

Dominic Cortez, Lunalilo Heights.

Dear Jesus:
On this Saturday morning, 2nd of November, I will open the day with a prayer to you, knowing the entire state is probably doing the same, so I completely understand if you don't reply right away… Jesus, there are certain things about this SB1 bill that extremely anxious and religious parents and teachers are not telling you. Before I proceed, I want to give you a brief introduction about myself, just so you know where I'm coming from. I'm an educator for 27 years. I received my M.A. in Sociology from U.C. Berkeley and my doctorate in Education from the University of Hawaii of Manoa. Regarding the concerns many parents have surrounding this bill and its effects on public education, I'd like to inform you that: 1) there's no portion in this bill that advocates for change in education curriculum. Such issues are handled by the Hawaii Board of Education and Department of Education, and their policy states that all curriculum must be standards-based. 2) As for sex education, Hawaii is an abstinence-based state, meaning we teach our students about abstinence as the best prevention and protection from pregnancy, infections, and diseases. And 3), should this bill pass—and most likely it will—parents will have the option, as they do now, to have their children not participate in such class discussion.

Amalia Buenaventura, P.Ed, Leeward Community College.

Dear Jesus:
"Love is an illusion created by lawyer-types to perpetuate

another illusion called marriage to create the reality of divorce and the need of divorce lawyers." Andrew McCarthy's character in *St. Elmo's Fire*.

Gordon Wong IV, a former Jehovah's Witness.

Dear Jesus:
The Hawaii Attorney General David Louie is for gay marriage. Twenty members of the State Senate are for it. The Department of Taxation and the Hawaii Civil Rights Commission are for it. The Department of Health, under Director Loretta Fuddy, is ready to issue marriage licenses to gay and lesbian couples. Is the fight over? No way, José, for outside the Capitol I hear the clamor of my brothers and sisters. "Let the people vote! Let the people vote!"

Charmaine Iwalani Vargas, Temple Valley.

Dear Jesus:
I'm anxious about the future of Proverbs 22:6 – "Start children off on the way they should go, and even when they are old they will not turn from it." If SB1 passes, there will be no way but to turn gay. Jesus, kill SB1 bill now before this gay plague kills us.

Sharlene Ogawa, Aiea.

Dear Jesus:
Whether this bill gets passed or not, I cannot, I repeat, I cannot honor such law. I don't care if they have to arrest or fire me from my State job. I love my job. The records show I excel at it. I love the law. I protect the law. But over my dead body if I have to abide by one that impinges on my religious beliefs. How disrespectful to my Almighty Father in heaven.

Albert Broadbent, President, State of Hawaii Organization of Police Officers.

Dear Jesus:
Why are there no lipstick lesbos or butchies with mullets or scandalous mahus in the Bible? Just whores, pricks, assholes and war-lovers. What happened to us being all equal in God's eyes? Not fair. Not fair.

Trinity, homeless.

Dear Jesus:
Knock knock?
Who's there?
Ima.
Ima who?
You mahu.
I not mahu. Maybe you the one mahu.
I no suck dick.
That's not what Kerwin tole me.
Bull-lie.
Afterschool. Behind Portable C. Five times Kerwin said.
So? He wen' suck me too.
See? I knew it.
Knew what?
Tell you tomorrow.
No. Tell me now.
K. Meet me at Portable C. Five minutes.
Four minutes.
Okay.

Dear Jesus:
I was tired of being an astronaut, so I told my mother I wanted
to be a lesbian, just like my Uncle J.R. So guess what she did?
She took me straight to Fantastic Sam's and ordered the barber
to make a mullet out of me. I cried the whole day, Jesus. I looked
so ugly, so white trash, like Miley Cyrus's father - and I'm not
even Haole. I'm Okinawan. I'm still crying, Jesus, and today is
already the third day. I begged my mom to shave it off, just shave
it off, please, Mom. She said no, because she said I looked good as
a lesbian, especially with my mullet. Jesus, if you love me, please
shave my head bald while I sleep. I promise I'm never going to
wish to be a lesbian again. Ever.
  Previn Higa, 9, Prince Kuhio Elementary.

Dear Jesus:
Is Mercury in retrograde again? Or is Venus in Uranus? Just

kidding.

Marty, Moanalua.

Dear Jesus:

I open today's Sunday paper to read about a teen who woke up covered in flames. He had dozed off on the school bus when his classmate, also sixteen, set him on fire. When asked why he did it, he said it was because the boy, after repeated warnings, continued to attend school in a skirt. Welcome to the future!

Julie Tadayashi, Kaimuki.

Dear Jesus:

I don't like the new blue M&M's. Can we let the people of Hawaii vote to abolish it?

Kelly Pacheco.

Dear Jesus:

In case the same-sex marriage equality bill no pass, can I, Bully Kupihea Jr., still be head cheerleader for the Kapa'a Warriors and wear my hot pants and do my Shakira-waka-waka dance routine during halftime? Love u 4-eva, B.K.J., Kapa'a High.

Dear Jesus:

I'm beginning to sound like a broken record. SB1 is not about what gets taught in classrooms. It's about the thousand-plus Federal benefits that, at present, are denied to same-sex couples. But since we're back on the topic of pedagogy, students discussing gay and lesbian characters in novels and short fiction don't turn them into raging fags and dykes, as someone argued in their testimony, just as learning about drugs won't turn you into an addict or a prostitute.

Amalia Buenaventura, P.Ed, Leeward Community College.

Dear Jesus:

Why don't they listen to me? I'm a millennial. My opinion matters the most. I am the future—bright, promising, full of hope. But if this bill passes the House, it's going to turn Hawaii into another Canada, where all public bathrooms are unisex. The

thought of sharing toilets with the
opposite sex is frightening. Worse, if it's with the same sex. Oppose SB1 bill NOW and save Hawaii from becoming the next Canada.

Linda, New Hope, Farrington High.

Dear Jesus:
When I grow up, I want to start my own ministry and be the first gay minister. I'll call it "New & Improved Hope" or "Hopelessly Devoteds."

Michael/Michelle, 14.

Dear Jesus:
Okay. Here goes. Please no mine my grammer, Jesus. I jus like share wit you my testamoney dat I goin' give at the State Capitol tomorrow. Like my Repretensative Mataele I only wen' go up to Turd World edumacation. But dis mo impotant. Now, you know me, Jesus, you know I no mo nutting agenst gays. Lesbiyans I get plenny, but not mahus. Watever dey like do in da privasy of der own home, well, das der kuliana. I get plenny mahu freinds and I goin be one liar if I tole you I never explored der dark side of life. You alredy know dis I'm sure. My wife Marlene know too. As your Fada is my witnes, I no mo nutting for hide. My life just like one open book alredy. Stay short but true. If you read 'em, everything stay right der on da first page. Wat gets my goat is dat dem mahus and wahines who stay stiring up all dis cantroversy is sending one false mesage to our kekis. Dey argyu dat to be gay and lesbiyan is not a choise. I agree. Das why leopards get spots, yeah? I know hard for dem to be like dat. I know not easy for dem to put up wid discremanation. But wat I like know is if dey know dat alredy den why stoke da fire even more? Why even bring up kekis in dis world? Besides, the world alredy made in China! Dont dey know dat wats hard for dem going only be harder for der children? But dey no can see wat I see becuz dey not part of da lite. In regardless, dis dey should tink about real hard. Sending dem my prayurs, Jesus. Peace. Love.

Willy from Maunawili.

Dear Jesus:

Shame on Representative Mataele2. Does he even know what "conscientious objectors" mean? Or is he just quoting phrases from the Constitution, Chapter 5, Verse 33.6? Didn't he flat-out told the molecular biologist Dean Hamer that he should be spoken to in lay lingua because he'd only received a Third World education? Does he know - or is he even aware - of the repercussions of such remarks? Which Third World is he referring to? Hawaii? Brigham Young University? Or his worldview?

Kaipo Williams, Waimanalo.

Dear Jesus:

I been waiting since Thursday to give my testimony. It's now Monday, November 4. I already missed two days of work. Might not seem much to the average Joe Blow, but that's gas money to a North Shore guy like myself who has to drive 15 miles into town so I can afford to eat at McDonald's three times a day. And it's not like I can just up and leave the State Capitol because if I not here when they call my number - 3,405 - they'll skip me as if I never paid my annual taxes, which means I'll have to get another number and miss more days of work, and if that's how it's going to be, then the State should make up for my lost income because they're the one who called this special session from out of the blue, I mean, everything was quiet on the North Shore front until they pulled this stupid stunt on us.

Marlon, Sunset Beach.

Dear Jesus:

Janina here. Freshman lipstick lesbo from Kahuku High. Just found out Cover Girl discontinued their Bistro Burgundy line. SOS.

Dear Jesus:

Did I hear it right? Did he or didn't he - a cop AND the President of the Organization of Police Officers - just swore that if this bill gets passed, he is willing to lose his job, get arrested or be killed, as it would turn him from a law enforcer to a lawbreaker? Talk about shooting one's self on the hoof!

Joni Chinen, Ala Moana

Dear Jesus:
Many homos believe we at New Hope hate them. Please. The world doesn't revolve around them. There are more crucial issues in this world than seeing two men or two women exchanging vows at the altar, like organ trafficking and global child prostitution. Plus, it's not as if they were born-again yesterday! Spare us the melodrama.
Moses Cabral, Moanalua.

Dear Jesus:
Do you think James P. Kealoha who sits behind me in Algebra and copies my homework is bi-curious? If you think so, can you relay a message to him from me: I think he's jalapeño-hot and that I wouldn't mind losing my divine virginity to him. Tell him I can host at my house from 7 a.m. to 10 p.m. but not later than that because that's when my mom usually comes home from her second job. Jesus, if only I had a va-j-jay I wouldn't be doing this.
Anonymous, 13, Damien High.

Dear Jesus:
Tell Hawaii to hurry it up. Illinois just beat Hawaii as the fifteenth state to legalize gay marriage. Plus General Motors is extending marriage benefits to spouses of same-sex employees. Not that I'm gonna quit my City & County job as a liquor commissioner and go work for GM in Michigan or wherever their factory is. I'm not gay, lesbian, transsexual, or bi-curious. I can't even recall the last time I had sex. And this is not by choice either. Sad face to be placed here.
Peace, Nolan Kimura, C&C of Honolulu, Liquor Commissioner.

Dear Jesus:
Kauikeaouli, or Kamehameha the III, who was the son of King Kamehameha I, also had several aikanes. From what I hear, he and his lovers, like Kaomi and Keoniana, put the cowboys in *Bareback Mountain* to shame. The king was so taken by Kaomi's good looks - he was part-Tahitian and part-Hawaiian, that he was

willing to make him co-rule his kingdom. But Chief Kaomi died - cause: unknown - shortly before their conjugal governance could be realized. Another lover of King Kamehameha III was Keoniana - or John Young II - whose father, John Young I, was a Scottish military advisor who also happened to be an aikane of Kamehameha I. Talk about a lineage of kings with male lovers. Irony of ironies: although King Kamehameha III practiced aikaneship, he was the first king in the Hawaiian monarchy to reject polygamy and follow the Christian tradition of marriage to only one woman.

Mililani Silva, curator, Bishop Museum.

Dear Jesus:
I am a girl who loves other girls but the commercial with you in it says it's wrong. What if I ask for another vagina? One for the right reason and the other for the wrong. That way, it's fair and square, as my teacher says. Right? So please give me another vagina. I'll be waiting for it by the Likelike overpass.

Yours truly, Sam(antha), 3rd grade, Kalihi Elementary School.

Dear Jesus:
Kindly convince the seven UNDECIDED legislators to vote YES to same-sex marriage so that my Aunt R.J. can finally marry Tita M.C. who's living in the U.S. illegally. They've been together for five years. Tita M.C. is Aunt R.J.'s caregiver. Yup, they're old but not old enough to, you know, enjoy each other, if you know what I mean. Their five years of "friendship" is more than all the years of marriages combined in our family. If this law doesn't get passed and if this prayer winds up with INS, then Tita M.C. will most likely be deported back to the Third World, or "Turd World"—that's what she calls the Philippines. I don't know. I've never been there. But if you end Third World now, then Tita M.C. will go home, knowing the economic conditions will be better with high employment rate. Though it would mean breaking up with Aunt R.J., unless she moves to Manila with her.

Lois Cabradilla, Hilo High.

Dear Jesus:

My traditional parents change religion faster than their underwear. In one month, we went from New Hopeless to Word of Lifeless. Then we switched to Catholicism b/c my mother found out from my Auntie Eileen that the new pope wears Prada and Gucci. Then we switched to Pentecostal because my parents think they can sing and faint at the same time. Now, my father wants to be a Mormon b/c, he says, a traditional father should have five desperate wives per household. Vote YES to traditional family.

Jonah Asuncion.


Dear Jesus:

Why they picking on my cop cousin, calling him any kind names, like his brain is one major pain in the ass? Excuse me, anatomically speaking, the brain stay way at the top, while the pain is at the bottom of things. And for your information, dumb and dumber are two people, my cop uncle, who heads the union, get only one mind and one body! Besides, everyone is entitled to his and her opinion, right? My cop uncle/union leader only exercising his. To those who don't like it, I say: WHATEVS!

Princess, La'ie.


Dear Jesus:

I so embarrassed, so humilahated. My faddah wen' go State Capitol yesterday for give his testimony. He waited 11 days cuz he was number 10,348, which was an exaggeration (he was 4,038). He a member of New Life in Leeward. Before that, New Word in Windward. And before that - he was incarcerated at OCCC for 2 years for aggravated assault and chronic road rage. He said he not proud of what he did but he said everybody get skeletons if you dig deep enough. If gays have their walk-in closets why shouldn't he? He told all this on Olelo LIVE STREAMING. He also said he pro-traditional family. He told the legislators he been w/ my maddah for 16 happily years. He was in 11th grade and she, 8th. They been happily married for 7 years since they joined New Life. He get three happy children ages 16 (me), 13 (brother), and 12 (sister). Jesus, if you do the math, it no add up.

It means my maddah is not my maddah and the maddah I have now got pregnant soon after she met my faddah. Right? So, I like know now: who is my maddah?

Diane Carvalho, Kapahulu.

Dear Jesus:

I failed you. I'm sorry. After waiting for what seemed like eternity, I was finally asked by Rep. Sylvia Luke to approach the mic and begin my two-minute testimony. "Aloha," I said. "Aloha," the committee members answered back. Next thing I knew - nothing. I couldn't get a word out. It was as if my tongue had been chopped off. A minute went by and, still, not a single sound or syllable. I held my palm out. I tried to tell the committee members through my facial expression that something was happening to me, that the god of scissors had entered my body and cut off my voice. Look at me! Can't you tell something is wrong? my face was shouting to them. But I got no reaction. They probably thought I was just another lolo old lady who'd gone to the State Capitol to waste two minutes of their time, like the woman who used up her time shouting "Let the people vote!" or the Born-Again singing "Amazing Grace" with a thick Korean accent. It was not until tonight, when I tuned in to watch the news and saw myself as one of the highlights from today's testimonies. Apparently, I couldn't only produce a sound out of my big Portuguese mouth, but I was also denied the right to emote. On my face was a huge blank, like I had been injected with a gallon of Botox or something. Only after my two-minute was up was I able to comprehend what happened. That was when I lost it. Completely. I started shouting uncontrollably "Maluhia, maluhia" - which means "peace, brother, peace, sister." I was so far gone I had to be escorted out of the building by three bodyguards to the jeers of my Christian brothers and sisters.

Failure Marie Machado from Hana, Maui.

Dear Jesus:

Feels like Day 357 of same-sex equality debate. Shet, this freakin' bill feels like a trial that's taking longer than O.J. Simpson's and Roe Versus Wade's put together. Even Jeffrey Dahmer's case was shorter than this; his only lasted two weeks. And by the looks of it, this trial might go unresolved, like the murder of Jon Benet Ramsey. I just hope that the HPD will be at the Capitol till this thing blows over. Would like to see that Samoan cop doing his job, though, that is, protecting everyone, including those law-abiding same-sex loving tax-paying citizens he abhors, who are helping pay his salary.

'Til Tomorrow, Lex.

Dear Jesus:

Today, Tuesday, November 5th, has got to be the most depressing day of the year. The joint House committee voted 18-12 in favor of this same-sex marriage bill. I don't know how these 18 legislators can go to sleep tonight, knowing the majority of the people of Hawaii are against this bill. Now, it's goes to the rest of the House to vote.

Disappointed Richard, Maile.

Dear Jesus:

No let this stupid bill pass. I no like be educamacated about mahus and lesbos. Get enough of them on TV, like Kirk and that black tranny; they both on *Glee*. Neil Patrick Harris, the Doogie Howser guy, I know he gay in real life but he okay because he play straight in *How I Met Your Mother,* plus he get one star on the Hollywood sidewalk. And no allow teachers for edumacate us about Adam and Steve in the classroom, Eve and Liv too.

Mahalo. J. T., Hawaii Baptist Academy.

Dear Jesus:

My testimony was short and simple. I just wen' read them my tattoo on my right arm. Leviticus 18:22. "Do not have sexual relations with a man as one does with a woman; that is detestable."

Jeremy, Papakolea.

Dear Jesus:

Before we continue our relationship, I only ask for one clarification. Exactly which side of hope are you? Are you with New Hope or the old one, because if you converted to the new one, then I want to know what was wrong with the old one? If the old hope is no good precisely because it's old, then that means that, sooner or later, this new one will eventually be of no use because it too will eventually age. If this is the case, are you then telling me that hope is like a loaf of bread: it has an expiration date. Once it expires, it will grow moldy, rot, disintegrate, et cetera - and then what? Newer Hope? Redux Hope? Latest Hope? That said, I'm still hopelessly devoted to you.

Alice Pacheco, Kahuku (by the old sugar mill)

Dear Jesus:

Representative Jo Jordan, who is part of the Finance committee and who, as everyone in West Oahu and Club Rose knows, is an out-and-proud lesbian (if her mullet isn't a dead giveaway then I don't know what is). Anyway, she voted NO. I repeat: a lesbian lawmaker voted against gay marriage. Thank you, Jesus. There is hope at the end of the rainbow. Jesus loves you Rep Jo, mullet or no mullet.

Virgie Lacaran, Waianae.

Dear Jesus:

My name Xian Lim. I Chinese defective now living in Hawaii five years. In Guangdong, China, where I from, we don't allow this kind marriage between same sex. If civet cats, okay, because they full of SARS, but not humans, especially lady to lady. It's not right. I not hateful type, but it's not Christian. Peace Always.

Dear Jesus:

Can you please tell those brainiacs like that chromosologist from Harvard for stop picking on Representative Mataele and making him look like one laughing stock west of Kahala? He ain't one baboon, babooze, he one human being, too, like John "The Elephant Man" Merrick! So what if he only went to Leeward Community College and gotta be spoken to in 3rd grade layman-Pidgin when explaining that homosexuality is in the DNA? Genetic or not, my pastor disagrees, ergo I disagree with him. And even if it is, it no mean that once a gay, always a gay. Get plenty ex-gays that I know in my Bible studies group. I

255

believe it all boils down to "choice," and they come in A, B, C, D, or E. That's why it's called "multiple"! Hello?! At least now, he represents the Micronesians in the Kehii Lagoon district, which he wen' achieve through hard work, perseverance, and prayers. Remind them that, Jesus. Choice first before genes.

Braddah Al, Ewa Beach & Iroquois Housing.

Dear Jesus:

When you get a chance, please pass this message on to that man who read a Leviticus verse from his shoulder. Leviticus 19:28: "Do not cut your bodies for the dead or put tattoo marks on yourselves. I am the LORD." Mahalo.

Dear Jesus:

For days, Mary, I was at the State Capitol today for check out the drama. Mary, was so nails. Wen' feel like I was watching one C-rated camp flick. But guess who I saw making all that "Let the People Vote" noise pollution around the Father Damien statue? Efren Lopez, the biggest Filipino bakla in the history of Waipahu High. You remember him? Muffyrella used to wear choke obake cosmetics and went around saying he hapa when he one flat-out flat-nosed Ilocano from Sarrat. Well, I guess he had a bad case of epiphany because he was acting all straight at the State Capitol (more like scared-straight). He was so convincing I almost never recognized him if not for his crater face. He was tongue-twisting with the other drama-sci-fi-comedy queens. For real kind, Mary. If that's what tickles his okole, then let him. I waiting for that day when all these self-hating mahus come out of the closet. This island probably going sink. So maybe they better not, yeah?

Trixie, Hotel St/Bethel.

Dear Jesus:

We have one more chance to kill this bill. Please try and persuade the remaining twenty-one representatives to vote NO on this bill. The pro-gay marriage only needs 26; they already got 18. That's only 8 votes shy from making our nightmare their reality. Jesus, time to walk on water.

Kenneth Pang, Kalama Valley.

Dear Jesus:

Oh, my god, what is happening to our dyke from Waianae? Has she gone back to the closet? Hope not. We hope sister C.J. will change her mind and vote YES tomorrow. Please do not let her make the wrong decision that will affect her future relationship with the gay and lesbian community in Hawaii, especially with the 500 active members of LOVE (Lesbians Organizing Vanguards of Eros), which she is a part of. Guide her, oh Lord, in these next twenty-four hours, and remind her to base her decision not on whom she is representing but on what she stands for and believes in. We pray she will reverse her NO to a YES.

Hoping, 500 members of LOVE.


Dear Jesus:

We did it. The House voted 30-18 in favor of Senate Bill 1. Three abstained because they want to be re-elected by their constituents. The House is taking a day off tomorrow from the public, then resume on Friday for the final history-making vote. I shall always remember today, Wednesday, November 6, 2013 as a date worth memorizing. I don't know if you have anything to do with this victory, but thank you anyway. Sorry to take up so much of your time. I'm sure you're up to your neck with prayers and complaints this very minute.

Maxwell of Ala Wai Apartments in Waikiki.


Dear Jesus:

Tell your ministers they got no business meddling in the same-sex marriage bill because their churches aren't paying taxes. In fact, they're abusing their non-profit status. Bad enough they're holding their ministries in public school grounds where Church and State should not be coupling. And until they start paying taxes, like the rest of us citizens, religious organizations have no say in this bill nor in any legislative bill, for that matter. We gays and lesbians have put up with bullying from your (make) believers for too long and are tired of being victims and sacrificial lambs. No more. Discriminate us, don't marry us in your churches, we don't care. Push comes to shove, we all know money speaks faster

than faith.
Isaac, Makiki.

Dear Jesus:
If Hawaii becomes the next state to legalize same-sex marriage, terrible consequences will follow such as global warming, widespread meth use (We're already in the Top 5), more power plant explosions such as that in Fukushima, extinction of endangered species, killer viruses, etc. etc.
Pastor Paolo, Whitmore Village.

Dear Jesus:
Another major dilemma-rama. For tomorrow's big event at the Capitol: 6-inch stilettos or slippers? Slippers, yeah? Easier for kill roaches with and going get plenty of 'em tomorrow. But for sure, I going wear my Kermit-the-frog-Rainbow-Connection-inspired tube top and the Jurassic organic hibiscus I bought for choke dollars at Wholefoods that I going wear behind my left ear. I going squeeze myself back into my 35-year-old Calvin Klein jeans cuz I no like nothing come between me and my you-know-what, except Russell Teruya (and maybe Shawn Ebisu). I going decorate my kino with body glitter for that Lucy-in-the-sky-with-diamonds effect. And, last but not the leastest, Love's Baby Soft perfume cuz innocence is sexier than you think (unless you getting harrassed on the bus by freakin' psychos and pervs). My look going be so retro but still about aloha and ohana. Cannot wait for tomorrow already. I going shine. Real shine.
Heavenly yours, Janice Kawehionalani Lee.

Dear Jesus:
Who cares about the final vote on Friday, the 8th? The end of the world is already here, and it's heading towards the Philippines. Forget us, Jesus, we can manage. They need you more over there.
Librado Encarnacion, Waihawa.

Dear Jesus:
If you're not going to let the Representatives let us, the people, vote, then we're not going to pray for you. Deal?

The Mob-ettes outside the Capitol.

Dear Jesus:

"Let the people vote! Let the people vote!" Uhm, they already did, and they're called General and Primary elections. What a bunch of nimcompoops! This is an issue of minority civil rights. It cannot be decided by the majority. If it were up to them, U.S. History would be a blank slate. Women wouldn't be voting right now. Schools and public restrooms would remain segregated. Rosa Parks would still be riding in the back of the bus. African American slaves would, well, still be praying for the freedom train. Inter-racial marriages would be banned. So, yes, let the people vote and let's return humanity back to the black hole.

Gary Kurishege, History Professor, U.H. Community College, Diamond Head Campus.

Dear Jesus:

First, I want to tell You how truly remarkable You are for putting up with all the BS and other blasphemous things that are being said about You lately, especially from the other camp. I wish I had Your patience and tolerance. Second, You are probably aware of this individual (local? Haole?) who is currently collecting letters addressed to you and posting them on his (her?) FB page. His/Her FB page is "Dear Jesus." It's the one with the profile pic of a Hawaiian monk seal These letters are either in support of or against same-sex marriage. According to him/her, no alterations were done to favor one side over the other, that they were posted immediately upon receipt. I don't know what his/her objective is but, to me, these postings achieve nothing except to mock those who are fighting to protect their religious beliefs as well as their constitutional right to Freedom of Speech. I am also concerned with his/her inclusion of letters from children, many of them expressing their pro-stand on same-sex marraige. These children are lost, Jesus. They have fallen out of touch with You. They will grow up on the margins of society, be cast aside and treated like lepers, prostitutes, addicts, and terrorists. They will lead undesirable lifestyle, participating in unhealthy activities that will certainly lead to their demise. Guide them back to Your

temple, Jesus. Let these millennials know that there's still hope.
  Sincerely, Anna D.

P.S. I have a strong suspicion that this letter collector is a disgruntled kamaaina (possibly a haole?) who used to be a minister or an active member of our ministry.

Dear Jesus del Mar:
I am your namesake, a stovepipe sponge of the phylum porifera, meaning "pore bearer". To the majority of sea creatures, we are nothing but pores and channels and have been repeatedly accused of making waves because of our phallic shape. We're thick, long, and open to whatever the tide brings to us. I am praying to you because, recently, I have fallen in love with Joao, a Portuguese man-of-war from Waimanalo. Like myself, it too is supposed to be asexual. But, love, as they say, works in mysterious ways, even for self-reproducing species like us. Since we started dating, we have been bullied, ostracized, threatened, particularly by sponges and jellyfishes in the Kingdom Hall of Animalia Witnesses. They've charged us of tampering with Nature, a crime comparable to first-degree manslaughter where, if found guilty, we will spend the rest of our lives in exile, in either the Atlantic or Indian. SOS, Jesus.
  Praying and poring, S, off of Hanauma Bay.

Dear Jesus;
We are now officially back in pre-1954 segregation era. At the Capitol the Mauka, or mountainside, of the rotunda is for those in favor of same-sex marriage; the Makai, or seaside, is for the opponents. Along Beretania Street, the pros can wave at motorists on the left side, same side as the Father Damien statue; the antis on the right side. Both sides also have separate entrances to the gallery, as well as their pre-assigned elevators, Fire Exits, water fountains, and soda vending machines. Pink trash cans with pink triangles on them are for pro-equality, and those against it are marked with black crosses. McDonalds have also been kind enough to accommodate both sides. Those in support can dine at the McDonald's in Fort Street Mall, and those against it can

go to the one on Beretania, across the Honolulu Academy of Arts. As for parking, the pro's can use any metered parking along Richard Street and the ones along Punchbowl are designated for the antis. Metered parking along South King Street is on a first-come first-serve bases. Do not park at the post office or at the State building or your cars will be towed, regardless of your stand on the issue.

Sadly yours, Dominic Corpuz.

Dear Jesus:
2 much H8 n da 808. Peace. Luke.

Dear Jesus:
Wow! I never knew get so many frigging drama queens on this island. Watching the hearing on TV was like watching one bad soap opera without a cliffhanger, like *Dynasty* without Alexis Carrington Colby Dexter. I was expecting fights for break out, bitches for get into a hair-pulling tag team match. But nothing. The best ones was that lady from Maui who wen' into catatonic state and the Bozos in our government - O.M.G.! Like the representative from Waimanalo who wen' equate the passing of this bill to 9/11. WTF, right? That's almost like me comparing the hearing to the Jim Jones Guyana tragedy. But, eh, this our fault; we the ones who wen' elect these baboons. We deserve it! We should pop a bunch of Ambien or Dramamine pills and, who knows, maybe by the time we wake up from our deep slumber, Hawaii going be a paradise in Mars.

Marty, Mililani Mauka.

Dear Jesus:
Just requested Rep. Chris Lee (hunk times ten, and those six-pack abs!) to be my friend on FB. Hope he confirms.

Charlene Kobayashi, 35.

Dear Jesus:
Are you behind—or an accomplice to—the creation of some of these state representatives? Please say no. They make the twisted characters in David Lynch's *Twin Peaks*, Oliver Stone's *Natural*

*Born Killers*, and John Waters' early flicks, the ones starring Divine, normal. One just out-channeled Ann Coulter. Another used the platform to poorly imitate Glenn Close in *Damages*. Then there's the wonder duo who should just deactivate: the Hawaiian version of Sarah Palin and the Tongan representative who "received a Third-World education" in BYU (his exact words, not mine) who confuses democracy with anarchy. Not to forget the legislator who sounds as if he was born out of a karaoke bar in Koreamoku. Please say you had no role in their genetic and psychological make-up.

Awaiting your YES or NO reply, Allan (two "L's" followed by an "A." Allan, not Allen.    Allen is Woody, mine is African-American, like Allan Houston, no relation to Whitney, no relation to Eli. The world is small but we're not all related, you know).

Dear Jesus:

Regarding Representative Lulu Mae Kahele from the Big Island—kindly teach her the proper use of symbolism. Her use of a bag of rice to signify a Hawaiian cultural staple is just wrong and an insult to the Hawaiian people that she claims to belong to. Shouldn't it be a bag of poi, kalua pork, pipikaula? And, correct me if I'm wrong, Jesus, but isn't this bill about same-sex marriage equality? How is this related to the legacy of colonialism? Is she operating on Hawaii Standard Time or still trapped in the vog zone of Kona? If my friend Ku'ualoha, who is Hawaiian, goes into convulsions because of Lulu Mae's convoluted definition of Hawaiian culture and identity, I'm going to blame it on her. Also, remind her to stop saying she supports equality and the LGBT community, because, obviously, she doesn't. And if I can make one last request, remind her she is a representative in Hawaii State Capitol and not at the Kodak Theater attending an Academy Awards ceremony. She turned her argument into a tireless Oscar "thank you" speech. What film is she nominated for? "A Day in the Life of Sam, the Spam?"

Just my two cents, Lucky Machado, Ph.D, English Renaissance Lit.

Dear Jesus:

Please take Representative C.J. Judas and each and every silver strand of her mullet with you. We never asked her to be our poster child. She has turned her back on the LGBTQ community in favor of what she calls her "conscience." Did her conscience tell her to deny people like us equal rights, too? Turncoat! We don't need another Benedict Arnold. She can rest assure that she won't be invited to any of our ceremonies, celebrations, cookouts, and Trivia Pursuit night.

Signed, 500 members of LOVE.

Dear Jesus:

END OF THE WORLD x 2 '30 YES's, 19 NO's, 2 CHICKEN SHITs.

Lala Bushwell, E.R., Queen's Medical Center.

Dear Jesus:

I have been up since midnight, watching and listening to lawmakers vote YES or NO to a bill that will determine an integral part of my future. A right that shouldn't have been debated over, challenged, or suppressed in the first place. Fortunately, there are more than enough representatives who share the same viewpoint. Tonight, they voted and, for the first time in Hawaii's history, handed me my long overdue rights. It is now 3:30 in the morning. There is still time left to pick up the remains of a dream and let it roam with other mysteries before it returns to whisper, "There. We're almost there, you and I. Goodnight for now."

Yours Truly.

# CONTRIBUTORS

**Mojisola Adebayo** (BA, MA, PhD, University of London) is a performer, playwright, director, producer, workshop leader and university lecturer. She has worked worldwide in theatre, television, radio, community arts and education, for twenty-five years, from Antarctica to Zimbabwe. Her own plays in production include *Moj of the Antarctic: An African Odyssey* (Lyric Hammersmith and Oval House), *Muhammad Ali and Me* (Oval House, Albany Theatre and National touring), *48 Minutes for Palestine* (Ashtar Theatre and international touring), *Desert Boy* (Albany Theatre and national touring), *The Listeners* (Pegasus Theatre), *I Stand Corrected* (Artscape, Oval House and international touring), and *The Interrogation of Sandra Bland* (Bush Theatre). Her publications include several of her performed plays in *Mojisola Adebayo: Plays One* (Oberon Books), *48 Minutes for Palestine* in *Theatre in Pieces* (Methuen), *The Interrogation of Sandra Bland* in *Black Lives, Black Words* (Oberon Books), *The Theatre for Development Handbook* (Pan, co-written), plus numerous academic chapters.

**Jess Arndt** received an MFA at Bard and was a 2013 Graywolf SLS Fellow and 2010 Fiction Fellow at the New York Foundation of the Arts. Arndt's writing has recently appeared in The LA Review of Books, Lithub, Hazzlitt, Fence, BOMB, Night Papers and the art journal Parkett, among others. Their debut story collection, *Large Animals,* came out on Catapult Press in May, 2017. Arndt is a co-founder of New Herring Press and lives in Los Angeles.

**Jay Bernard** is a writer, film programmer and archivist from London. They recently worked on Regina V Turing and Murray, a 360° film experience with the National Trust and as a programmer at BFI Flare, co-curated Year Dot, an exhibition and symposium around queer technology. Jay is the author of four poetry pamphlets, including *The Red and Yellow Nothing* (2016), a queer-techno-medieval misadventure which was shortlisted for the Ted Hughes Award for new work.

**Richard Brammer** was born in 1975 and resides in Manchester,

UK. For a while he wrote a lot of books all at once where the words didn't go all the way to the end of the line. Then he wrote not so many books and the words did go to the end of the line. His latest book *The End of History* (Dostoyevsky Wannabe X) is about gynaecological laboratories and Northern Soul. He's a co-founder of Dostoyevsky Wannabe.

**Victoria Brown** was born in 1978 in the North of England. She is a co-founder of Dostoyevsky Wannabe. She has written one book of poetry, *Cherry Bomb* (2015). She may, at some point, finish her second book, 150 Pornographers. She is allergic to cats.

**Steven J. Fowler** is a writer and artist. He has published multiple collections of poetry and been commissioned by Tate Modern, BBC Radio 3, Tate Britain, the London Sinfonietta, Wellcome Collection and Liverpool Biennial. He's been translated into 22 languages and produced collaborations with over 90 artists. He is the founder and curator of The Enemies Project, editor at 3am magazine, lecturer in creative writing at Kingston University, teaches at Tate Modern and is the director of Writers' Centre Kingston.

**Juliet Jacques** is a writer and filmmaker. In addition to publishing two books, *Rayner Heppenstall: A Critical Study* (Dalkey Archive, 2007) and *Trans: A Memoir* (Verso, 2015), her fiction, essays and journalism have appeared in Granta, The Guardian, The London Review of Books, Sight & Sound, Frieze and many other publications. She lives in London.

**Sara Jaffe** is a fiction writer living in Portland, OR. Her novel *Dryland* was published by Tin House Books in 2015. Her short fiction and criticism have appeared or are upcoming in publications including Catapult, Fence, BOMB, NOON, The Offing, and The Los Angeles Review of Books. She co-edited *The Art of Touring* (Yeti, 2009), an anthology of writing and visual art by musicians drawing on her experience as guitarist for post-punk band Erase Errata. She is currently working on a collection of short fiction entitled *Hurricane Envy*.

**Roz Kaveney** is a poet, novelist, critic and activist living in East London. Among her books are the poetry collection *Dialectic of the Flesh*, the critical collection *Reading the Vampire Slayer* and the *Rhapsody of Blood* fantasy novels. *Cream Whip* is a projected sequel to her Lambda-Award-winning novel *Tiny Pieces of Skull*.

**R. Zamora Linmark** is the author of four poetry collections, including *The Evolution of a Sigh* and, most recently, *Pop Vérité*. He has also published two novels - *Leche* (Coffee House Press) and *Rolling the R's* (Kaya Press), which he'd adapted for the stage. Forthcoming is *These Books Belong to Ken Z* (Delacorte/ Random House), his first YA novel. His latest play *But, Beautiful* will have its premiere in 2019, in Honolulu. He currently resides in Manila and Honolulu.

**Mira Mattar** writes prose and poetry. She is a contributing editor at Mute and co-runs a small press. She recently edited the first critical anthology on Chris Kraus, *You Must Make Your Death Public: A collection of texts and media on the work of Chris Kraus*, and co-edited *Anguish Language: Writing and Crisis*. She lives in south east London. Some of her work can be found here: http://hermouth.tumblr.com/ @hermouth

**Seabright D. Mortimer** is a writer interested in queer and trans narratives. Their work has appeared in The Guardian, Vice and DIVA magazine. Recent explorations include a tract on queer internet time and black holes in the writings of Stephen Hawking and the paintings of Caravaggio. They recently completed three new poems as part of a project funded by the AHRC and their short story *Thumbs in Space: Love in The Age of Likes* will be published in 2018. A longer work all about salmon, gender and queer ageing processes is on the horizon.

**Nat Raha** is a poet and trans/queer activist, living in Edinburgh, Scotland. Her poetry includes two collections *countersonnets* (Contraband Books, 2013) and *Octet* (Veer Books, 2010); and numerous pamphlets including *de/compositions* (Enjoy Your Homes Press, 2017), *£/€xtinctions* (sociopathetic distro, 2017), '[of sirens / body & faultlines]' (Veer Books, 2015) and *mute exterior intimate* (Oystercatcher Press, 2013). Nat co-edited the *Radical Transfeminism* zine, and is currently finishing a PhD on queer Marxism and contemporary poetry at the University of Sussex.

**Nisha Ramayya's** poetry pamphlets *Notes on Sanskrit* (2015) and *Correspondences* (2016) are published by Oystercatcher Press. Her writing can be found in Ambit, Datableed, Litmus, Poetry London, and Zarf. She is a member of the Race & Poetry & Poetics in the UK research group and she teaches Poetic Practice and Creative Writing at Royal Holloway, University of London.

**Rosie Šnajdr** is a writer and academic. She co-edits the Cambridge Literary Review. Her short story collection *A Hypocritical Reader* is published by Dostoyevsky Wannabe.

**Timothy Thornton** is a writer, composer, and performer. He makes queer stuff about ghosts, foxes, birds, and the sea, and lives in Brighton.

**Isabel Waidner** is a writer and cultural theorist. She is the author of three books of innovative fiction, most recently *Gaudy Bauble* (Dostoyevsky Wannabe, 2017), which the writer and critic Olivia Laing described as a "beguiling, hilarious, rollocking and language-metamorphosing novel". *Gaudy Bauble* is currently longlisted for the TLS-sponsored Republic of Consciousness Prize for "hardcore literary fiction and gorgeous prose". Waidner's articles and short fictions have appeared in journals including 3:AM, Berfrois, Configurations, The Happy Hypocrite, The Quietus and Minor Literature[s]. As part of the indie band Klang, she released records on UK labels Rough Trade (2003) and Blast First (2004). She is a lecturer in Creative Writing at Roehampton University in London, and the editor of *Liberating the Canon: An Anthology of Innovative Literature* (Dostoyevsky Wannabe, 2018).

**Joanna Walsh** is the author of seven books. The most recent, *Worlds From The Word's End*, was published by And Other Stories in 2017. In 2018 *Break.up* will be published by Semiotext(e) in the US and Tuskar Rock in the UK. Her writing has appeared in many journals and anthologies including Granta Magazine, and The Dalkey Archive's Best European Fiction. She edits at online literary journals 3:AM Magazine and Catapult, writes literary and cultural criticism for an number of publications including The Times Literary Supplement and The Guardian. She founded and runs @readwomen, described by the New York Times as "a rallying cry for equal treatment for women writers." She is the UK Arts Foundation 2017 Fellow for Literature and the 2018 Burgess Fellow at the Anthony Burgess Foundation, Manchester.

**Eley Williams** is a writer and lecturer based in Ealing. Recent publications include a poetry pamphlet *Frit* (Sad Press, 2017) and collection of stories *Attrib. and other stories* (Influx Press, 2017). The latter was listed among the best books published in 2017 by The Guardian, The Telegraph and The New Statesman and chosen by Ali Smith as one of the year's best debut fiction.

37316852R00160

Printed in Great Britain
by Amazon